ECONOMIC AND SOCIAL COMMISSION FOR ASIA AND THE PACIFIC

FOCUS ON ABILITY, CELEBRATE DIVERSITY:

Highlights of the Asian and Pacific Decade of Disabled Persons, 1993-2002

Social Policy Paper No. 13

UNITED NATIONS

New York, 2003

ST/ESCAP/2291

UNITED NATIONS PUBLICATION
Sales No. E.04.II.F.7
Copyright © United Nations 2003
ISBN: 92-1-120360-0

MAY 18 2004

FOREWORD

As we enter the first year of the renewed Asian and Pacific Decade of Disabled Persons, 2003-2012, it is fitting that we celebrate some of the success stories of the first Asian and Pacific Decade, 1993-2002. This first Decade, which concluded in December 2002, was a unique initiative of the United Nations Economic and Social Commission for Asia and the Pacific. The Asian and Pacific region was the first and only region in the world to take up the challenge and promote a specific regional initiative, following the conclusion of the first Decade.

In the revitalization of ESCAP, which I have undertaken during the past three years, the work focus has been redirected to address three critically important themes: poverty reduction, managing globalization and emerging social issues. Poverty is a multidimensional issue and the links between disability and poverty are well-documented, with the World Bank suggesting that persons with disabilities may account for as many as 20 per cent of the world's poorest of the poor. The ESCAP commitment to emerging social issues has always been rights-based and people-focused. This approach underpinned the focus of the first Asian and Pacific Decade of Disabled Persons, as we have witnessed a marked shift in attitude during the last 10 years from a charitable and welfare-oriented approach to one firmly based on human rights and development. One of the key issues currently being addressed by ESCAP, as we enter the first year of the second Asian and Pacific Decade of Disabled Persons, is mobilizing active regional support for the proposed United Nations Comprehensive and Integral International Convention on Protection and Promotion of the Rights and Dignity of Persons with Disabilities.

The title of this publication, with its very positive emphasis on ability rather than disability, and on the celebration of diversity rather than the exclusion of those perceived as 'different', reflects some of the very significant achievements of the Asian and Pacific Decade of Disabled Persons. An earlier publication, *Pathfinders: Towards Full Participation and Equality of Persons with Disabilities in the ESCAP Region,* formed part of the rigorous evaluation of the first Decade. The publication was prepared for presentation at the High-level Intergovernmental Meeting, convened in October 2002, at Otsu City, Shiga, Japan, to conclude the Decade. Together, the two publications form a valuable record of some of the very successful initiatives that have taken place in countries and areas of the ESCAP region. They demonstrate the many ways in which the quality of the lives of women and men, and girls and boys, with disabilities has improved during the Decade. They also reflect the actions taken that will benefit many more persons with disabilities in our region in the future.

It is my hope and belief that the stories and case studies presented in this volume may provide inspiration to others, thus spreading the impact to reach the millions of disabled persons not yet reached by the benefits experienced by the many whose rights were upheld, equality of opportunity enhanced and lives enriched as a result of the implementation of the first Asian and Pacific Decade of Disabled Persons.

KIM HAK-SU
Executive Secretary

December 2003

CONTENTS

CONTENTS *(continued)*

CONTENTS *(continued)*

ANNEX

ASIAN AND PACIFIC
DECADE OF DISABLED PERSONS, 2003-2012

BIWAKO MILLENNIUM FRAMEWORK FOR ACTION:
TOWARDS AN INCLUSIVE, BARRIER-FREE AND RIGHTS-BASED SOCIETY
FOR PERSONS WITH DISABILITIES IN ASIA AND THE PACIFIC

CONTENTS *(continued)*

Figures

INTRODUCTION

The Asian and Pacific Decade of Disabled Persons, 1993-2002, proclaimed on 23 April 1992, by means of the United Nations Economic and Social Commission for Asia and the Pacific resolution 48/3, has ended. The achievements of the Decade have been subjected to a rigorous process of evaluation, involving United Nations agencies, Governments and non-governmental organizations, including organizations of persons with disabilities. The formal review process indicated that significant progress had been made in many policy areas of the Agenda for Action for the Asian and Pacific Decade. The policy areas included:

- National coordination
- Legislation
- Information
- Public awareness
- Accessibility and communication
- Education
- Training and employment
- Prevention of causes of disability
- Rehabilitation (community-based rehabilitation)
- Assistive devices
- Self-help organizations
- Regional cooperation

An earlier publication, *Pathfinders: Towards Full Participation and Equality of Persons with Disabilities in the ESCAP Region,*[1] formed part of the evaluation of the Asian and Pacific Decade of Disabled Persons. It was prepared for presentation at the High-level Intergovernmental Meeting convened in October 2002, in Otsu, Shiga, Japan, to conclude the Decade. Pathfinders presented examples of good practice toward the achievement of full participation and equality of persons with disabilities. The case studies reflected achievements in nine of the policy areas of the Agenda for Action.

The title of this publication, *Focus on Ability, Celebrate Diversity: Highlights of the Asian and Pacific Decade of Disabled Persons, 1993-2002* reflects its purpose. Amongst the most significant achievements of the Decade has been the positive shift in attitudes towards persons with disabilities and the increased awareness, acknowledgement and celebration of their diverse abilities. This has been accompanied by the realization that further progress cannot be made unless it is within a human rights framework, that disability issues must be addressed in full consultation with persons with disabilities themselves, and that the concerns of persons with disabilities should be included fully in all mainstream national development agendas.

---

[1] ST/ESCAP/2170.

At the fifty-eighth session of the Commission a resolution was adopted by member Governments proclaiming the extension of the Decade for a further 10-year period, from 2003 to 2012. The progress of the first Asian and Pacific Decade had exceeded expectations but it was clear that there was no room for complacency. Progress was uneven, and in most places from a low baseline. Significant changes in attitude, in acknowledgement of the rights of persons with disabilities, still have to be translated into continued action, in order for persons with disabilities to achieve full empowerment. At the High-level Intergovernmental Meeting to Conclude the Decade members adopted the Biwako Millennium Framework for Action towards an Inclusive, Barrier-free and Rights-based Society for Persons with Disabilities in Asia and the Pacific (BMF). This is the policy framework that will guide Governments and their partners in implementing actions to achieve the goals and targets of the renewed Decade.

The Biwako Millennium Framework has identified seven priority areas for action:

- Self-help organizations of persons with disabilities and related family and parent associations
- Women with disabilities
- Early detection, early intervention and education
- Training and employment, including self-employment
- Access to built environments and public transport
- Access to information and communications, including information, communication and assistive technologies
- Poverty alleviation through capacity-building, social security and sustainable livelihood programmes

It is clear that certain important trends and issues have emerged during the latter stages of the first Decade, including increased attention to the issues of women with disabilities, early detection and intervention for infants and very young children with disabilities, and information and communication technology (ICT), as well as the realization that the challenges of poverty and disability are inextricably linked. Some of these areas are well represented in the case studies presented in this volume.

This publication is a celebration of innovation, dedication and outstanding achievement. It reflects activities undertaken at national level, and subregional and regional initiatives, particularly in the development of self-help organizations, the first and foremost priority area of the BMF. It describes the work of committed self-advocates, many of them graduates of ESCAP training programmes, two of whom have received regional and international recognition for their advocacy work with prestigious awards bestowed on them. Examples of good practice have been presented from Bangladesh, Cambodia, India, Indonesia, Japan, the Oceania Pacific subregion and Samoa, Thailand and Viet Nam.

This publication also provides an avenue for sharing ideas and experiences. It is hoped that dissemination of these examples of good practice will inspire others to action across the region, as we enter the early stages of the second Asian and Pacific Decade of Disabled Persons. ESCAP wishes to thank all those who have contributed the stories of their work, and of the people they have worked with, to be included in this commemoration of the conclusion of the Asian and Pacific Decade of Disabled Persons, 1993-2002.

PART ONE

SELF-HELP ORGANIZATIONS

I. Overview of Self-help Organizations

I t is perhaps of symbolic importance that in the Agenda for Action for the first Asian and Pacific Decade of Disabled Persons, the policy category of self-help organizations was 11th out of 12 policy areas. In the Biwako Millennium Framework for Action, the policy document and guideline for the renewed and extended Decade, self-help organizations is the first of seven priority areas identified for particular emphasis and action during the period 2003-2012. While policy areas have not been deliberately ranked in order of importance, it does reflect a shift in attitude. Disability issues are no longer considered to be the primary concern of service providers for persons with disabilities, perceived as passive recipients. Instead the slogan of Disabled Peoples' International (DPI) "nothing about us without us" has come closer to being a reality.

In the review of achievements at the end of the first Decade, DPI membership included 23 national assemblies in 23 countries, with several more in the process of formation. The World Blind Union and the World Federation of the Deaf have extensive networks of national organizations in the region. Governments were beginning to recognize the importance of self-help organizations and to provide support for their formation. Input by self-help organizations into national policy development was reported by 17 Governments.

The BMF states clearly that persons with disabilities are the most qualified and best equipped to support, inform and advocate for themselves and other persons with disabilities. Their input into the proper design and implementation of policy, legislation and strategies will ensure their full participation in social, economic, cultural and political life and enable them to contribute fully to the development of their communities. Communities which encourage this process will in turn be enriched. The targets of BMF demand support for the formation of democratic, cross-disability organizations which represent disabled people in rural and urban areas, and at all levels from grass-roots to national and regional level, and their full inclusion in decision-making processes.

The case studies presented in this section provide examples of national level action, as well as subregional and regional level action. In the examples from Bangladesh and Cambodia particular emphasis has been placed on engaging persons with disabilities at the grass-roots level. The focus is on advocacy and empowerment, building capacity to participate in planning, decision-making, implementation and management. A third of the countries and territories of the UNESCAP region are small island states in the Pacific. The DPI Oceania Office is only three years old. However, it has already provided significant leadership and undertaken systematic action to support the first steps towards development of strong national self-help organizations in the Pacific subregion. The number of national assemblies established has increased from four to seven. The other focus has been on building an effective networking system, capable of overcoming distance and isolation in remote locations. This has been very successful. The World Federation of the Deaf has proved the value of developing strong national organizations, based on the unique world view of the "deaf community". They extended their influence and experience to stimulate and strengthen self-help activity in deaf communities in less developed countries of the region.

II. Developing Role Models and Resources: Self-determination in the Pacific

A. Nature of the problem

Disability services were introduced to the Pacific between the 1960s and 1980s. This saw the establishment of numerous single and cross-disability non-governmental organizations in the Pacific subregion. The year 1981 was named the International Year of Disabled Persons and Disabled Peoples' International (DPI) was formed in the same year. Despite these promising initiatives, awareness of the disability movement and self-help organizations of persons with disabilities has remained minimal in the Pacific, particularly in the smaller developing island nations.

Traditionally, disability organizations have focused on delivery of services and been managed by non-disabled persons, adopting the view that persons with disabilities must be cared for, protected and segregated. Persons with disabilities were regarded as recipients of goodwill and unable to make their own choices or determine their own destiny.

Another hurdle in the self-determination of people with disabilities is culture, perceptions and attitudes. These attitudes can act as barriers to the participation of persons with disabilities in affairs that concern them, especially at decision/policy-making levels. The strong extended family system in most countries in the Pacific encourages family members to look after their own sick or less fortunate relatives. The association of a disabling condition with ancestral curse, parental misdeeds, witchcraft, shame and fear keeps persons with disabilities isolated, neglected, dependent and poor. Furthermore, the struggling economies of these island nations also inhibit government attention to the presence, needs and concerns of their disabled population. The disabled population is a minority group in most cases and their needs are outweighed by the national priorities and agenda.

Further, the ability of self-help organizations to campaign for the rights and needs of the disabled to be put higher on the national agenda is hampered by lack of coordination between the many self-help groups, and their often limited focus and resources.

The challenge to persons with disabilities in this subregion is to work towards gaining greater recognition and support for their involvement in decisions and activities that affect their lives. This involvement can be within their local communities, national governments or even management of disability organizations. This involvement is essential if they want to play a more active and leading role in affairs that concern them. This task can only be accomplished if people with disabilities are given equal treatment and opportunity, and are empowered, motivated and equipped with relevant information, skills and experience. Thus, the establishment of the DPI Oceania Subregion Office in Suva, Fiji in 2000 was significant as it acknowledged the self-determination of persons with disabilities in the subregion.

B. Main features of the organization

The DPI Oceania Subregion is one of the five subregions of the Asia-Pacific Region which in turn constitutes one of the five regions of DPI. DPI is an international cross-disability, self-help, human rights organization of people with disabilities and represents a relatively new social movement with member organizations in 114 countries worldwide. DPI was founded in 1981, during its First World Congress held in Singapore at the end of the ground-breaking United Nations International Year of Disabled persons (IYDP) prescribed for the same year. It endeavours to promote and achieve the goal of human rights for people with disabilities. Full participation in society, equality of opportunities, and self-directed developments of persons with disabilities are its major objectives. DPI's philosophy provided the basis for the United Nations World Programme of Action Concerning Disabled Persons through such principles as human rights, full participation, self-determination, integration and equalization of opportunities. On 17 August 1987, the United Nations gave DPI a testimonial award for dedicated service in support of the United Nations World Programme of Action Concerning Disabled Persons which served as the basis for implementing the United Nations Decade of Disabled Persons, 1983-1992. From the beginning, DPI's strategy in achieving its goal has been empowerment of people with disabilities through the building up of their individual capacities and their self-help organizations in all parts of the world, especially in developing countries. In this way, they become effective advocates on their own behalf and are able to undertake their self-development.

The DPI Asia-Pacific Region has 22 member countries. Regular communication and close collaboration are maintained between the Oceania Subregion Office and member countries as well as with the Regional Office in Bangkok. Disability organizations as well as government departments and civil society organizations that provide disability services in countries of the subregion are being identified and encouraged to recognize and support the full participation and equal treatment of persons with disabilities. To fulfil its vision, the Oceania Office organized the first subregional leadership training seminar in Port Vila, Vanuatu in August 2001. National leadership and empowerment seminars were planned for Papua New Guinea and Samoa in 2002.

C. Achievements

Prior to its establishment, only four countries were recognized by DPI to have set up national self-help organizations of persons with disabilities in the subregion. These are Australia, Fiji, New Zealand and the Solomon Islands. All four have become member national assemblies of DPI. After its establishment phase spanning a period of six months from March to August 2000, the DPI Oceania Subregion Office, through the financial support of the Nippon Foundation of Japan, continued to strengthen its position, develop its role and raise its profile in the Pacific and beyond. Four key areas were targeted by the DPI Oceania Office to guide its strategic goals and objectives. These are:

- Capacity-building
- Profile raising
- Networking
- Increasing membership

The first Oceania subregion leadership training seminar was held in Vanuatu in August 2001 and attended by about 40 persons with disabilities from nine countries in the subregion. This seminar was instrumental in obtaining support from the Government of Vanuatu and has raised the profile of the issue of disability in the broader community. The Disability Promotion and Advocacy Vanuatu (DPA) has expanded in membership and has formed close and positive links with other disability-related and civil society organizations. DPA Vanuatu obtained full membership of DPI at the DPI Regional meeting held in Shanghai, China, in October 2002.

The Oceania Disability Advisory and Support Committee (ODASC) was also formed at this leadership training seminar in 2001. This committee was set up in response to the need for persons with disabilities from participating countries to support, communicate and network with each other to promote and strengthen the disability movement in the subregion. As a result of this, a subregional network of self-help organizations has been formed in Vanuatu, Samoa and the Cook Islands. These countries are now seeking membership in DPI.

In August 2002, the second Oceania Subregion leadership training seminar was held in Lae, Papua New Guinea. Papua New Guinea has the largest population of any Pacific Island country, in excess of five million people. It is further challenged by its mountainous terrain, many remote communities, poor infrastructure and communications systems. Formation of a strong organization of persons with disabilities has been hampered by poor communication, lack of resources and the fact that disability services have been dominated by non-disabled people. The Leadership training seminar had very significant results. In August 2002 the National Assembly of People with Disabilities, (NAPD Papua New Guinea), was formed, and was accepted as the formal body to represent persons with disabilities in Papua New Guinea at the DPI regional meeting referred to earlier. Thus, the disability movement in Papua New Guinea has developed impetus and begun activities to advocate for disability legislation and to undertake extensive awareness raising activities and extension of the NAPD to provincial level.

The overall goal of the Leadership Seminars is to provide an opportunity for international learning experience and exchange for leaders who have disabilities from Asia and the Pacific islands. Furthermore, it assists in building and strengthening individual and organizational capacities, and strengthening the network of organizations in the region. Hence, it enables people with disabilities to be able to promote and achieve for themselves full participation, equality and integration within their own societies, and allows them to contribute constructively to their nation's development effort.

The Oceania Office has not limited its activities to the workshops and seminars which it has initiated, but has responded to requests for support of initiatives and activities at national level from several countries and territories in the region. In March 2001 the Ministry of Internal Affairs, focal point for disability in the Cook Islands Government, conducted a historic workshop entitled "The Cook Islands Disability Council Establishment and Awareness-raising Workshop", with funding assistance from New Zealand Overseas Development Aid. The Workshop had the express purpose of establishing the Cook Islands Disability Council and, just as importantly, of raising awareness concerning disability issues amongst Government personnel, people from the wider community and people with disabilities and their families and caregivers. These objectives were achieved, and a series of recommendations for immediate further action made. These very successful outcomes were in part due to the vital input of the Oceania DPI Subregional Coordinator, Mr Setareki Macanawai, whose exceptionally high level of technical expertise, combined with his inspirational advocacy have earned him acclaim beyond the Oceania subregion.

The Cook Islands became a signatory to the United Nations Economic and Social Commission for Asia and the Pacific "Proclamation on the Full Participation and Equality of People with Disabilities in the Asian and Pacific Region" on 19 July 2000. In signing the Proclamation, the country was also party to the adoption of the "Agenda for Action for the Asian and Pacific Decade of Disabled Persons, 1993-2002". The Cook Islands took these commitments seriously and has proceeded to take many actions resulting in the finalization of the Cook Islands National Policy on Disability and Action Plan, in June 2003. This document may provide a valuable model for other Pacific countries embarking on these steps. The progress in the Cook Islands has been achieved with very close consultation, cooperation and support from the DPI Oceania Office.

In May 2002 a similar exercise was undertaken in Samoa, again with support from the Oceania Office. A national association of persons with disabilities was formed and in October 2002 in Shanghai, China, both the Cook Islands and Samoa national assemblies were accepted into the DPI family.

The participation and involvement of persons with disabilities as resource persons in disability related seminars/workshops have also been acknowledged, promoted and practiced in the subregion as in the case of Vanuatu and Cook Islands in 2001. This was also the case in Samoa, Solomon Islands and Papua New Guinea in 2002. The experience and leadership of the Fiji Disabled People's Association have been prominent and valuable in this initiative. Through the hard work of the Oceania Subregion Office, there has been a marked increase in the participation and representation of persons with disabilities, related organizations and relevant government departments from the subregion in regional and international meetings pertaining to disability. Furthermore, the Oceania Office has promoted disability issues as an important agenda for such Pacific-based regional organizations as the ESCAP Pacific Operation Centre, the Pacific Islands Association of Non-governmental Organizations (PIANGO), the Pacific Islands News Association (PINA) and others.

D. Key lessons learned

Even though the Oceania Subregion of DPI Asia-Pacific Region has been in existence for some time, the actual setting up of the DPI Oceania Office occurred in March, 2000. Therefore, key lessons learned are based on experiences, activities and feedback in the past three years.

Information sharing, communication and networking help improve and strengthen disability organizations in Pacific Island countries. Within the short period since DPI Oceania's establishment, there has been an increase in information pertaining to disability which the DPI Oceania Office has disseminated to these countries. Such information empowers disability organizations and motivates disability workers to learn and find out more about disability issues to make their services more effective and beneficial to the various target groups they serve. Also, most of the countries are at a similar level of disability development and exchange of experiences, success stories and newfound knowledge aids progress in throughout the region.

Persons with disabilities are good role models, effective advocates and valuable resource persons. Much has been achieved in the area of self-help, self-determination and empowerment of persons with disabilities in this subregion because the DPI Oceania Office actively involved capable and successful persons with disabilities from Pacific island countries in its training programmes. The establishment of self-help organizations in Cook Islands, Samoa and Vanuatu are direct outcomes of such initiatives. Countries in the Pacific subregion share similar cultures, lifestyles and challenges, which enable persons with disabilities to identify with each other and draw strength from each other's experiences.

Non-governmental organizations are largely responsible for services to persons with disabilities in the Pacific subregion. From the contacts DPI Oceania has established with countries and territories in the subregion, it is evident that governments in almost all of these countries played a limited supportive role by way of minimal grants. This support is only forthcoming if funds permit. Policy support is also limited by the formulation of policies driven by social or economic reasons rather than human rights and equity issues. Yet, despite government reliance on NGOs to provide much needed services, their contributions are often ignored or overlooked. NGOs must be recognized, not just by their governments, but by international organizations such as ESCAP, the World Bank and Japan International Cooperation Agency (JICA) as valuable partners in any disability development initiative in this subregion.

Persons with disabilities must be empowered, trained and supported to play more active and leading roles in disability programmes in their respective countries. DPI Oceania Office has discovered that for the most part, persons with disabilities in this subregion see themselves merely as recipients and beneficiaries of services provided by disability agencies. Positive self-esteem, self-worth, self-confidence and family/personal counselling are essential components of any intervention measure prior to the promotion and implementation of full participation and equal opportunity programmes.

E. Sustainability

The DPI Oceania Subregion Office is an important catalyst and change agent for and by persons with disabilities in the subregion. It currently enjoys the financial support of the Nippon Foundation of Japan and guidance of the DPI Asia/Pacific Regional Office in Bangkok. However, countries and territories in this subregion must be encouraged to support this project, as it plays a pivotal role in the promotion and recognition of the human rights of, and self-determination by, persons with disabilities. Furthermore, this disability movement must not be seen as a threat to existing disability agencies and related government programmes in the subregion. Rather, the primary role of the DPI Oceania Office is to complement and strengthen such services by sensitizing government leaders, civil society and management of disability NGOs to the rights and capacity of persons with disabilities as equal partners in any disability development initiative.

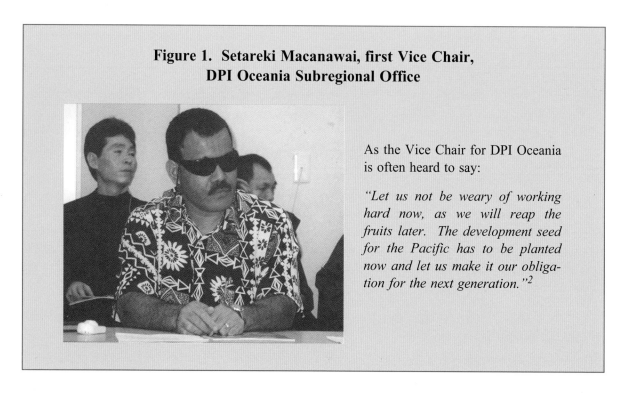

**Figure 1. Setareki Macanawai, first Vice Chair,
DPI Oceania Subregional Office**

As the Vice Chair for DPI Oceania is often heard to say:

"Let us not be weary of working hard now, as we will reap the fruits later. The development seed for the Pacific has to be planted now and let us make it our obligation for the next generation."[2]

---

2   Disability Oceania. Pacific Disability Forum. Vol. 3, Issue 1, page 3.

III. Towards Holistic Development: Capacity-building and Localization in Bangladesh

A. Nature of the problem

There are an estimated 13 million people with disabilities in Bangladesh and they are overwhelmingly poor. The link between poverty and disability is undeniable. However, little has been done in the way of systematically examining the linkages between the two. Disability is both a cause and consequence of poverty. The vulnerability of people with disabilities to poverty is multidimensional – impacting on their employment and income earning potential; they are often excluded from participating or taking up opportunities open to others; they are discriminated against at the institutional, social and cultural levels; and they are often marginalized or isolated within their own societies and families. Poverty reduction strategies and basic support services for economic development and capacity building for them is urgently needed. This includes localization of power and ownership of programmes and activities by people with disabilities and their organizations.

B. Main features of the organization

Bangladesh Protibandhi Kallyan Somity (BPKS) was established in 1985. BPKS is a non-governmental, voluntary organization of persons with disabilities in Bangladesh working to ensure equal rights, opportunities and participation of people with disabilities in mainstream development and decision-making. Such rights, opportunities and participation with give them the opportunity to play a responsible and contributive role in the community.

BPKS has designed and is implementing a development strategy entitled, *Persons with Disabilities' Self-Initiative to Development (PSID)*. This project is being implemented throughout Bangladesh using a human-rights-based approach. The activities under the project assist people with disabilities to organize and develop their organizations to provide traditional physical and mental therapy services and to attain economic advancement, equipment, accessibility and vocational training. They also provide services that increase the capacity of people with disabilities, thus assisting them to mainstream their needs and actualize the development process for all.

The priority goal of BPKS is to ensure that there is an innovative and inclusive process in place that utilizes the power and success of persons with disabilities to streamline and actualize national development for all. PSID is a timely process which empowers persons with disabilities, from the grass-roots level to the national level, to partake in a full, happy, dignified and productive life. PSID ensures the rights, the participation and the actualization of opportunities equally for all persons. PSID strives to eliminate prejudice, discrimination, inhumanity and lack of basic opportunities.

Under the direction and guidance of PSID Centres at local (subdistrict) levels, Self-Initiative to Development Units are established at grass-roots levels. Each Unit and its respective Centre undertakes a three-year implementation phase during which BPKS provides organizational and financial support. During this time members are provided with the necessary skills to manage and further develop their organizations on a self-sustaining basis. Once ownership is handed over to the people with disabilities themselves, BPKS continues to provide technical support including training, information, coordination and technical assistances to the grass-roots organizations. At this point the entire project is fully localized, with the leadership of the organization assuming full responsibility for all financial and programme management. At this stage the organizations gain their own individual legal status and registration to ensure independence. Each PSID project area then becomes known as Disabled Peoples' Organization to Development (DPOD), customized to recognize local ownership at the district or subdistrict level to include the district name preceding the title, for example *Kurigram Disabled Peoples' Organization to Development (KDPOD)*.

The strategy of the Self-Initiative to Development Units is as follows:

- Needs assessment

    A baseline needs assessment survey is conducted to identify the location of people with disabilities, with whom they reside and their circumstances. Once individual needs and disabilities are identified, a detailed monthly plan is developed for the field. For each new area, BPKS directly works with an average of 2,500 people with disabilities.

- Develop skilled persons (service providers)

    Skilled service providers from the community provide home-based therapy, assistive devices maintenance support services and regular referral services for health and preventative measures.

- Enrolment of children with disabilities in general education

    This is encouraged by conducting counselling with family and communities. It is also pursued through lobbying and advocacy with education authorities, orientation training for teachers to learn teaching techniques on disability, incentive considerations to install ramps in schools, adaptive materials, tuition and nutrition allowance.

- Facilitate and develop economic opportunities for people with disabilities

    This is be done through weekly savings plans, home and/or community-based income-generation skills training, income-generating activities, access to local financial institutions, job placement, tree saplings, and loan support from the savings and Program Acceleration Fund (PAF).

- Access to a safe environment

    Safe environments are created by installing safe, accessible sanitary latrines and tubewells, as well as orientation training on hygiene and safe environments.

- Increase self-respect and capacity

    This is done by ensuring grass-roots organizations are adequately developed and managed. Strong grassroots organizations should have the capacity to accelerate programmes, provide leadership, and understand the importance of lobbying and advocacy, self-confidence, gender equity, country status, accessibility and localization of power training.

- Research, organize and network

    Lobbying and advocating at local and national levels and educating and motivating the relevant government and non-government agencies, engineers, architects, physical planners and development partners is carried out. In addition, the printing and dissemination of community education materials, development of audio-visual materials, organization of campaigns and utilization of mass media materials should be undertaken.

- Engagement as an activist and consultant agency

  This can be done at the national, regional and international level for government, non-governmental agencies and donors.

- Sharing of lessons learned

  BPKS has shared the system for development and management of the self-help organizations by making its PSID policy available to ADD and ActionAid Bangladesh. The PSID system has also been shared with Caritas-Australia, Australian Volunteers International (AVI), AusAid, USAID, European Commission, Bread for the World (BftW), CordAid, One Family International (OFI) and many others.

- Sustaining the progress

  BPKS must continue to set up permanent facilities as a focal point of disability by establishing a training and resource centre at Dhaka (BPKS Complex) and at the local level (district and subdistrict). It must mobilize local resources, both financial and in-kind, to support the activities of coordination, professional capacity building and skills training. Networking, human care and referral, assistive devices production, information and referral, setting and conducting meetings, employment exchange, and marketing of products made by persons with disabilities should also be conducted.

- Network and coordination systems developed

  This should be done at national and grass-roots levels, consisting of self-help organizations, women with disabilities, health professionals and facilities, government departments and services, non-governmental organizations, other disability organizations and private business organizations.

C. Achievements

Significant results have been achieved by BPKS both prior to, and since the introduction of, the PSID project in 1998. Prior to 1998, about 10,000 persons with disabilities benefited directly from BPKS services. By the end of the year 2002, 38,556 people had been added. With the inception of the *Persons with Disabilities' Self-Initiative to Development,* 12 new self-help organizations have been established since 1996. There are now 7,840 individual members enrolled and responsible for each organization. Policy, skills and resources are transferred and localized to people with disabilities and their respective organizations, giving them the ability to manage and run their activities.

Localization of power, programme and ownership by people with disabilities has been achieved by the development of each organization and extensive capacity building. People with disabilities now serve as the organizers and decision makers, and as community and disability leaders. They are also responsible for providing services, and give voice to their success in actualizing and accelerating the overall development of the nation.

The programme approach has developed a systematic process of awareness building about disability among the general public as well as people with disabilities themselves. This in turn has helped mobilize local resources. PSID ensures the building of capacity to develop, provide, supervise and monitor skills training that ensures the stability of the services. In addition, studies on disability and development issues are conducted to measure and ensure the sociocultural viability and appropriateness of the programme.

Members associated with the self-help organizations develop their own resource base, composed of savings, management and development funds, utilizing these resources for their income-generating activities and the further development of self-help organizations and networks.

D. Key lessons learned

Persons with disabilities are directly involved in planning, decision-making, implementing and managing the organization and the PSID programme – from the grass-roots level to the national level. In essence, they own the organization and are fully responsible for it. Economic empowerment is an important component of PSID for people with disabilities who face many challenges in a country with extreme levels of poverty.

Positive behavioural change within communities is beginning to take hold, resulting in greater opportunities for education, employment and leisure activities. These changes in thinking, attitudes and practices pave the way for integration of people with disabilities into mainstream community life, stimulating the self-initiatives of people with disabilities to improve the quality of their lives with support and technical cooperation of local self-help organizations.

This two-fold developmental approach succeeds by focusing both on people with disabilities and their growth, as well as the changes within the community, thus assuring both internal and external strength. As people with disabilities become more self-confident and attain increased skills, they gradually ensure full access and equal rights in their societies, which substantially changes the perception and resultant acceptance. No longer will "disability" equate with "difference", and the commonality of human beings, both those with, and those without visible disabilities, will be accepted.

E. Sustainability

BPKS views sustainability in four areas – management, technical, knowledge-based and financial. Additionally, however, behavioural change in communities and understanding of people with disabilities is a sustainable requisite for full integration of people with disabilities into society. All BPKS senior management staff are locally hired, most with disabilities themselves. This reality has helped ensure management sustainability for the agency.

BPKS will continue to improve and expand its PSID programme until every district has active and successful self-help organizations, with people with disabilities retaining control and direction of their organizations.

BPKS will continue to:

- Promote the rights of people with disabilities;

- Support the development of expanded and more accessible opportunities for people with disabilities to improve their own quality of life;

- Raise awareness other development agencies on issues related to the needs of people with disabilities;

- Provide technical cooperation in networking, coordination, fund-raising, sustainability, poverty reduction and strengthening the capacity of people with disabilities and their organizations;

- Support advocacy activities for the inclusion of people with disabilities in national development plans and strategies; and

- Seek opportunities to share the PSID model with other countries.

As indicated in this case study, BPKS has achieved the significant goal of assisting people with disabilities integrate into society and increase their visibility within their communities. This visibility has the wider effect of engendering a more positive understanding in the community in general, lessening negative and anti-social attitudes and behaviours, while providing a role model for others to form their own institutions similar to the PSID project. With these realizations, there will be a shift from disability to the recognition of ability, both internally and within the wider community.

IV. Solidarity and Organizations of the Deaf in Asia and the Pacific

A. Nature of the problem

Until recently in the Asian and Pacific region, excluding Australia and New Zealand, there have been few deaf organizations that are autonomously managed, with a strong organizational structure, and performing significant activities. Establishing national organizations for the deaf is no easy task. The lack of such organizations in Asia and the Pacific does not detract from the solidarity of the deaf associations in the region. However, as the Japanese Federation of the Deaf (JFD) found through its early work in Japan, the driving force in achieving full participation and equality for people with disabilities is the organizations and movements of people with disabilities themselves. To achieve the important goal of consultative status with governments and to influence policy and decision-making in their own countries, self-help organizations need to address the issue of representation.

To assist in building the capacity of local organizations to come together and effectively advocate for the rights and needs of deaf people, JFD has focused its international aid programme on organizational support. It also drew on its past experiences in Japan to support other countries in the Asian and Pacific region to develop and strengthen their organizations and activities in the assistance of deaf people.

B. Main features of the organization

The Japanese Federation of the Deaf (JFD) is the only nationwide organization of the deaf in Japan. It is characterized by the use of sign language as the primary means of communication. JFD is a member of the World Federation of the Deaf (WFD).

With its headquarters in Sweden, WFD is an international organization of the deaf. Membership is restricted to one association of the deaf from each country. At present, 120 countries are enrolled as WFD members – 63 per cent of the 190 United Nations member countries. All WFD member associations use sign language as the means of communication, although the actual sign language used differs from country to country. The use of sign language is a binding force uniting the deaf associations of the world with a strong sense of solidarity. The "WFD Policy for the Work Done by Member Organizations in Developing Countries" sets forth the guidelines by which member associations give international support and aid. Article 2 states that projects should "be run by deaf people themselves – and in accordance with the organization's objectives and ethics".

Within Japan, JFD made great progress in improving welfare for deaf people through deaf rights movements conducted after World War II. Based on these experiences, JFD hosted the 9th World Congress of the Deaf in 1991 in Tokyo. The Asian and Pacific Decade of Disabled Persons presented another opportunity for advancement of deaf rights. As a member of the WFD, JFD has been playing an active role in helping to establish and develop deaf organizations in Asia.

By the end of the "United Nations Decade of Disabled Persons" in 1992, JFD had achieved some legal reforms in Japan, such as the amendment of Article 11 of the Civil Law, the amendment of the Traffic Law to enable the acquisition of drivers' licenses by deaf drivers, the establishment of a Sign Language interpreter system, although only in its early stages, and the passing of legislation to build "Information Centres for the Hearing Impaired". Although still far from achieving all of its goals, JFD and its deaf partners have been encouraged by these achievements to move forward toward "full participation and equality".

C. Achievements

1. Building regional capacity

JFD hosted the "Fifth Leadership Training of Asian and Oceanian Deaf Persons", under the sponsorship of the Japan International Cooperation Agency (JICA) from 3 October to 21 November, 1999 at JICA's Osaka International Centre. Since the inception of the programme, eight deaf leaders have been chosen every year from countries such as Cambodia, China, Malaysia, Mongolia, Nepal, Philippines and Thailand to participate. The programme and study tour demonstrates to the chosen leadership trainees the importance of a rights-based approach overseen by the deaf community itself.

The programme was initiated in 1995. By 1999, five courses had been conducted and 39 trainees had completed the course. Before this programme, training for persons with disabilities was largely based on the concept of protecting those with disabilities. There were very few programmes considering people with disabilities as direct beneficiaries of training. Most of the programmes were designed for education or rehabilitation specialists, and the organizations in charge of the training were specialized training institutions rather than organizations working for or involving deaf people.

2. The Asian Deaf Friendship Fund

Besides the aforementioned "Leadership Training of Asian and Oceanian Deaf Persons", JFD offers funding support to deaf associations of countries belonging to the Regional Secretariat in Asia-Pacific. Funding through the Asian Deaf Friendship Fund is offered to countries that have a well established local or national deaf organizations.

The Fund is also used to support the host country of the yearly Regional Secretariat in Asia-Pacific Representative Meeting. The first meeting of the Regional Secretariat was held in 1999. JFD places great importance on this meeting as an opportunity to develop inter-agency communication among the countries of Asia and the Pacific. Participating associations are continuing to increase in number. The meeting is significant in that it is not simply a meeting of the representatives of the member associations but is normally held in collaboration with the deaf society of the host country. Such an approach assists in developing community-based deaf movements in the host country, as well as the capacity of the national-level organizations.

JFD also provided funds for scholarships for Thai students in schools for the deaf through the Fund. At present, annual funding is provided for scholarships and management fees for 20 students attending the Nonthaburi School for the Deaf and Chiang Mai School for the Deaf.

3. Building local resources

The United States-based Gallaudet University is the only university in the world for the deaf, accepting deaf students from all over the world, and using sign language as the official language. As part of a research programme, it sent researchers to Thailand to conduct studies on Thai sign language. The challenge posed by sign language dialects, and difficulties involved in the implementation of a national standard Sign Language are particularly evident in Thailand, in part because of the relative size of the country and, secondly, because of deficiencies in the traffic and transportation systems, thus impeding exchange and communication among deaf people living in different districts.

The results of these studies led to the publication of "The Thai Sign Language Dictionary" (volumes 1 and 2) in 1990. While this was a great achievement, the dictionary was extremely costly and not suited to practical use as a textbook for sign language learners; further it was largely unused by either the deaf or the hearing. A need still remained for a Thai dictionary. Looking for assistance, the National Association of the Deaf in Thailand (NADT) asked JFD to provide support to help publish a version of the standard Japanese Sign Language (JSL) vocabulary textbook, "Watashitachi no Shuwa" (Our Sign Language).

In compiling the dictionary, the selection of signs and their approval by the local districts necessitated editorial meetings with a nationwide representation. This provided the opportunity for deaf organizations and communities from around Thailand to come together not only to discuss the signs, but also to network with each other and share their experiences, goals and achievements. A computer system for the selection of the signs to be included in the textbook was also developed. The editing process was not easy, but in September 1999, the much-awaited books (volumes 1 and 2) were published.

Ten thousand copies of each volume were printed. Results were reported to the Thai Ministry of Education and samples of the new books were presented. The ceremony to present the report and books was attended by the Deputy Minister of Education, who promised to have the new books used as textbooks in deaf schools. This promise has since been fulfilled.

This joint project was a new experience not only for deaf people and groups in Thailand, but for JFD and NADT as well. Results were extremely worthwhile in that the project not only involved material support but also created strong humanities.

The free distribution of volumes 1 and 2 throughout Thailand has been finished. Seminars for dissemination of the dictionary have been organized. Now NADT is working on the editing of volumes 3 and 4. Copyrights and publishing rights were handed over to NADT in the hope that they will be a source of income for NADT.

D. Key lessons learned

The most successful way to assist the deaf is to ensure that deaf people are the key participants and organizers of programmes and activities to assist in their empowerment.

The lack of participation of deaf people in assessment of needs for support and developing education programmes for themselves is largely responsible for misguided efforts to export "aid" to the deaf. A common example of this is the provision of second-hand hearing aids as an auditory assistant to deaf children attending school. With the exception of specialized schools for the deaf, almost all schools conduct teaching using the auditory oral method. In this sort of system, to raise the educational level as a whole, those lacking the ability to keep up with the system are left behind. Apart from the provision of hearing aids, there are no measures to assist deaf children. This is, in effect, a screening process and the deaf are most often screened out.

E. Sustainability

JFD's international cooperation activities are targeted towards deaf organizations in Asia. In sending international support, it is important to ensure that the project can be sustained and that it matches the needs of the deaf people of the country. As such, support is not always provided continuously. It is also important to recognize the general situation and ensure that those who follow on can pick up where earlier projects left off for an effective and organic continuation of goals.

A. Nature of the problem

Cambodia is a country struggling to recover from its violent past. Its recent history of war has contributed to the country's high number of people with disabilities. The fighting factions used landmines in an indiscriminate way, causing losses among the civilian as well as the military population. Landmines cannot tell the difference between the footsteps of a soldier and a child. Unexploded ordinance continues to threaten many communities. This, the lack of a basic, functional health care system; widespread poverty and lack of access to appropriate physical, vocational and economical rehabilitation has contributed to the marginalization of landmine victims and other people with disabilities.

A number of assessments have been undertaken on the situation of people with disability in Cambodia, but they have mostly been confined to the planning needs of the specific organizations which conducted the studies. The Ministry of Social Affairs, Labour, Vocational Training and Youth Rehabilitation (MOSALVY) collects statistics on some categories of disabilities but the use of the data is limited by inconsistencies in their collection. A more comprehensive situational assessment has been undertaken for the National Task Force on Rehabilitation.

According to data collected for the Asian Development Bank in 1997,[3] by conservative estimates, approximately 9.8 per cent of the people of Cambodia have significant physical or mental disabilities that limit their ability to function independently on a daily basis. This grim statistic means that Cambodia has one of the highest per capita populations of citizens with disabilities in the world. The reasons for such a high rate of disabilities are varied, but there are three main reasons – poverty, the breakdown of essential services and the presence of landmines – all the legacy of more than 20 years of conflict in the country.

Between 2 to 3 per cent of the population, or about one out of every 40 Cambodians, have physical disabilities. Among these are approximately 40,000 to 50,000 landmine survivors, many of them young men in their productive years. There are roughly 60,000 persons with paralysis from polio, 100,000 persons who are blind, and 120,000 persons who are deaf.

Statistics on the number and types of mental disabilities present in the population are not available; however, it is possible to get a rough estimate using international averages based studies that have been conducted in 40 developing countries. Applying these averages to the population of 11.43 million Cambodians, it is fair to expect that, at a minimum, there would the following:

---

[3] Dana Peedles, "Skills Training as a National Strategy for Poverty Reduction in Cambodia" (ADB, 1997).

- 102,000 to 178,500 mentally retarded children, (or 20 to 35 children per thousand children below age 18);

- 20,400 to 40,800 people with severe mental disorders (2 to 4 people per thousand);

- 154,000 to 408,000 people with epilepsy (14 to 40 people per thousand); and

- 306,000 to 1,530,000 with significant personality disorders (3 to 15 per cent of the population).

B. Main features of the organization

The Cambodian Disabled People's Organization (CDPO) is part of the worldwide network of disabled organizations known as Disabled People's International (DPI) and has as its mission the development of networks of people with disabilities to support, protect, serve and promote their rights, achievements and interests and enable their full participation and equality in society.

CDPO was established with support from DPI in September 1994 at a three-day seminar attended by people with disabilities from 13 provinces around Cambodia. DPI continued to support CDPO in the development of the organization, both on a technical level and by raising funds for the first two years of the organization. The DPI-Cambodia project featured below was completed at the end of 1996, after an evaluation that took place in September 1996. From 1996 to 2000, CDPO implemented two Plans of Action in order to reach its 10 long-term goals intended to increase the capacity of people with disabilities to access equal rights and opportunities and improve their quality of life through advocacy work, public awareness raising and community empowerment of people with disabilities. This was done through the development of a grass-roots movement of self-help groups of people with disabilities using the provincial capacity and representatives or networks.

CDPO's role is not to provide services or material benefits, but rather to represent people with disabilities and advocate for their interests and empowerment by building their own awareness and capacity. This role makes it unique in Cambodia.

CDPO has 1,110 full members and over 1,500 observers (waiting for formal approval of the leadership of CDPO) in 21 provinces of Cambodia. It has also established four chapters in Kampot, Banteay Meanchey, Svay Rieng and Kampong Cham provinces. The membership meets every two to three years in a National Assembly. At the National Assembly a nine-member Central Committee is elected to oversee the organization. There have been three National Assemblies and three central committee terms.

C. Achievements

CDPO has played an important role in the disability movement in Cambodia and has made significant achievements in a short period of time. It has a major role at the Disability Action Council of Cambodia (DAC) Executive and Advisory Committee and most of the sub-technical committees of the DAC.

DAC led the effort to draft legislation on the rights of people with disabilities, and helped make people with disabilities and others more aware of their rights. It has supported people with disabilities in their efforts to prove their abilities and has publicized their achievements. It has helped people with disabilities build confidence and become effective leaders and has assisted them to enter decision-making positions.

It is necessary to change attitudes and build confidence not only in people with disabilities but also in the communities they live in, at the grass-roots level. To change negative societal attitudes toward people with disabilities, CDPO has effectively used media techniques such as production of quarterly newsletters, annual posters and brochures disseminated and displayed at major events, as well as radio and campaign spots on television. It has also supported the establishment of the Blind Musical Band.

In addition, it played a major role in the development of sporting activities for people with disabilities, after the establishment of the National Paralympic Committee of Cambodia (NPCC) – which was established through its facilitation. It is also supporting an active group of women with disabilities to address their own needs and problems. All these initiatives are directed at the grass-roots level and have the potential to empower and change negative mindsets of people with disabilities and those around them. Increasing access to opportunities is not just about overcoming physical barriers, but overcoming psychological barriers. Advocacy efforts to change policy and attitudes within the government needs to go hand in hand with raising awareness of the rights of people with disabilities in communities, workplaces, social environments and families, and among those with disabilities themselves.

CDPO is moving towards increasing technical support and decreasing financial support to representatives of some provinces such as Kampong Spue, Kandal, Kampong Chhnang and Prey Veng. Increased technical support would assist them to manage their membership activities effectively, and encourage the development of self-help groups in these areas. At present, three self-help groups have been developed in Kandal, and two each in Kampong Spue, Kampong Chhnang and Prey Veng.

CDPO has established four chapters in Kampot, Banteay Meanchey, Svey Rieng and Kampong Cham. All four are fully operational. It is expected that a further four branches will begin operations during the programme period in Kandal, Kampong Chhnang, Prey Veng and Kampong Spue. Activities are already underway in identifying resource persons and provincial representatives for these provinces.

CDPO branches also work in collaboration with the PRC and CABDIC programmes in Kampot, Banteay Meanchey, Kampong Thorn, Takeo and Pursat provinces, and with Action on Disability and Development (ADD) in Kampong Spue and in Kampong Chhnang. In addition, CDPO is collaborating with the American Friends Service Committee (AFSC) in Sihanoukville. The figure 2 indicates the main areas of activities.

Figure 2. CDPO: type of activity by province

Provinces with direct work	Provinces with networks	Provinces with collaboration
1. Phnom Penh	1. Kampong Thom	1. Kampot
2. Kampot	2. Kandal	2. Kampong Thom
3. Banteay Meanchey	3. Pusat	3. Kampong Chhnang
4. Svay Reing	4. Kratie	4. Kampong Spue
5. Kampong Cham	5. Stung Treng	5. Takeo
6. Prey Veng	6. Seam Reap	6. Sihanouk ville
7. Kandal	7. Koh Kong	7. Pusat
8. Kampong Chhnang	8. Prah Vihar	
	9. Pailin municipality	
	10. Mondulkiri	
	11. Sihanouk ville	
	12. Takeo	
	13. Kampong Spue	

D. Key lessons learned

In Cambodia, the measurement of poverty is based on a poverty line that takes into account food consumption that provides at least 2,100 calories of energy per person per day and a small allowance for non-food consumption to cover basic living items like clothing and shelter. The nature of poverty in Cambodia has been identified as following:

- Impact of the Khmer Rouge regime and the legacies of war on the population

- Lack of opportunities, vulnerability

- Lack of access to public services

People with disabilities form one of the most vulnerable groups in Cambodia, and have very limited access to education, skills/vocational training, job placement, income generation opportunities and other social services. As a result, many are extremely poor. Income generation for people with disabilities thus not only contributes to a sense of dignity and self-confidence, it is also directly linked to poverty reduction and development. Many view disability as a condition of occupational disadvantage, which can and should be overcome through a variety of appropriate programmes and services. Equality of treatment, mainstreaming of training and employment opportunities and community involvement are central pillars of the multisectoral approach.

CDPO believes in the self-help concept as the solution to the disability issue. CDPO believes in beginning with empowering, both at the social and economic level, through the development of a grassroots movement of people with disabilities and self-help groups for people with disabilities. This approach needs to be combined with capacity building, using chapters and resource persons/provincial representatives and adopting a collaborative approach with partners and service providers.

By working directly with people with disabilities at the community level, CDPO brings about solutions to specific needs through self-help concepts and philosophy.

E. Sustainability

The overall programme objective is to empower people with disabilities by assisting them to develop awareness of the issues they face, to identify and access technical and training resources, and to solve their problems together in a spirit of solidarity through the formation of local, district and provincial chapters whose members can make confident decisions, take action and exercise effective demands. Such an approach builds sustainability into the programme.

Through specific objectives that focus on raising awareness of the issues, needs, skills and requirements of the disabled population at the individual, family and community level; promoting self-esteem and increasing the capacity of disabled people; promoting the reintegration of disabled people within the community and increasing their opportunities for employment; and encouraging the development of a referral system and linkages between people with disability in the community and the agencies providing family and community support, sustainability of the programme goals and the objective of independence and self-help of persons with disability is ensured.

PART TWO

WOMEN WITH DISABILITIES

VI. Overview of Women with Disabilities

Although gender dimensions for the implementation of the Agenda for Action for the Asian and Pacific Decade of Disabled Persons were adopted in 1995, the issues of women with disabilities were only addressed on a very limited basis during the first Decade. Although the Agenda for Action was adopted in the same year that the Fourth World Conference on Women was held in Beijing, the mainstream gender movement has paid scant attention to the situation and concerns of their disabled sisters. In the regional review of achievements of the Decade only nine Governments spontaneously made any reference to this neglected, marginalized and hidden group of persons with disabilities. Formation of networks of women with disabilities was reported in six countries and gender-inclusive policies in only three.

Disadvantaged through their status as women, and as women with disabilities, they are over-represented among those living in poverty. To a greater extent than is the case for boys with disabilities, disabled girls face discrimination within the family, are more likely to be denied access to nutrition, health care, education, vocational training, employment and income generation opportunities. They are routinely excluded from social and community activities and are more at risk of physical and sexual abuse. Girls growing up in rural areas are even more disadvantaged, illiterate and without access to information or services.

Stigmatized and rejected from earliest childhood and denied opportunities for development, girls with disabilities grow up lacking a sense of self-worth and self-esteem, and are often denied access to the customary roles of women in their communities.

Only in the final years of the first Decade was adequate attention paid to issues of women with disabilities by self-help organizations. Here again they had been discriminated against and under-represented. Access to leadership training and executive positions was limited and their issues did not form part of the advocacy agenda.

The BMF has very strong targets for achievement for women with disabilities in the renewed Decade. Anti-discrimination measures are required to safeguard the rights of women with disabilities. They should have equal representation on national self-help organizations, in all training initiatives and at all levels of management. They should also achieve membership in national mainstream gender associations.

After a hesitant beginning, a regional network of women with disabilities was formed in 2001, and a formal structure and constitution adopted in 2002. Regional Leadership training workshops are now conducted annually for young women leaders with disabilities by Disabled People's International (DPI) Asia-Pacific regional office. ESCAP too, is continuing a tradition started in 2001 of providing training for women with disabilities, with two workshops on women and disability held in 2003.

The case study presented from Mobility India describes many of the problems and the discrimination faced by young women with disabilities. The highlight of this story is the successful transition from most disadvantaged status to a successful, economically independent self-reliant status, valued by their families and the community, and demonstrating that they have the capacity to learn and successfully carry out jobs previously reserved for men. This sensitive work addresses disability and poverty, demonstrating that with careful planning, determination and training the link can be broken.

VII. Skills-based Training: Empowering Women in their Families and Communities

A. Nature of the problem

There are more than 40 million women with disabilities in India. Gender discrimination compounds the discrimination these women already face as people with disabilities. Many girls and women with disabilities live their lives in complete deprivation with a very little control over their lives, and totally dependent on their families. Most often, they are treated as helpless and unable to do anything either for themselves or for their family. In many families they are kept hidden so as not to damage the marriage prospects of their siblings. In addition, some members of society regard women with disabilities as bad women. Women with disabilities suffer doubly from being women and being disable. Women are most often the most neglected, marginalized and hidden group of people with disabilities. Yet issues concerning the situation of women with disabilities have received little attention from the mainstream gender movement.

Many families do not want to put their time or resources into the welfare of their children with disabilities as they are considered non-productive and unable to contribute to the family's needs or economic security. Their basic needs and rights – like healthcare, education, skills training etc., are not considered as important. The literacy rate of women with disabilities is very low as a result. Access to rehabilitation facilities is also very limited. Further, few women with disabilities choose to wear appliances, compared with men. The dominant presence of the male technicians in the field of rehabilitation is one reason for this. Women, particularly those from more traditional societies, find the measurement and fitting of aids often embarrassing and immodest. The lack of female technicians is therefore an immense hindrance to the achievement of mobility for girls and women with disability.

The challenges above are largely the result of negative cultural and societal attitudes rather than of the physical experience of a disability. Collecting data on how community attitudes impact on women with disability, and the specific nature of the challenges they face as a result, is an essential first step in changing these attitudes. Increased understanding of the situation and status of women with disabilities can also led to increased community pressure on governments to provide legislative and policy support to women and men with disability. With this as a goal, Mobility India, a Bangalore-based NGO, conducted a sample survey of women with disabilities in Bangalore. The survey reported the following findings:

- The majority of the women with disabilities live in poor and isolated conditions;

- The visibility of women with disabilities in the community is strikingly less than of their male counterparts;

- They are mostly deprived of their basic rights such as education, health care, skill training, employment, family life and other social services; and

- Very few women with disabilities partake in rehabilitation or use aids and appliances for their personal mobility.

In addition, the survey found that only 1 per cent of women make use of skills training opportunities provided by government agencies and/or NGOs. Further, most are trained in tailoring, candle making, book binding, basket weaving etc., trades which no longer have the potential to generate sufficient income to make them independent or self-sufficient.

The results of the survey highlighted the urgent need to find and create increased and more economically beneficial opportunities to mainstream girls and women with disabilities. It also highlighted the need for alternative vocational/skills training in which women could develop their potential and be assisted in becoming economically independent.

The dire findings of the survey provided the impetus for Mobility India's "Rehabilitation Aids Workshop by Women with Disabilities". The main objectives of the programme were to:

- Train women with disabilities in the manufacture and repair of rehabilitation aids and appliances so that more women technicians would be available to address the needs of women with disabilities; and

- Promote equality for women with disabilities, to become economically independent, self-reliant and integrated into the mainstream.

B. Nature of the organization

The Rehabilitation Aids Workshop by Women with Disabilities (RAWWD) is a group of young women aged between 20 and 25 years who have physical, mainly mobility impairment. The project started in 1996. Ten women with physical impairment were identified from lower income families. They were given mobility appliances to enhance their mobility and confidence. This was followed by a one-and-a-half year course in the production of mobility aids and appliances. After the training, the participants were assisted in finding employment or setting up their own workshop.

Figure 3. Prema, Anita and Chandrama busy in the workshop

Training was provided in all aspects of running a workshop – such as purchasing of machines and tools, raw materials, contacting hospitals and other private practitioners for clients, need assessment and taking care of the clients, keeping accounts and all other related matters.

After completion of the training, Mobility India continued to provide technical support and additional on-the-job training to further develop and advance the women's skills. In just two years the workshop became self-sustaining. The women trainees established good relations with hospitals and private practitioners (the main source of clients), and became proficient at procuring raw materials for making the appliances, conducting regular follow-ups, keeping records of the clients, maintaining accounts and other related tasks.

The increased income and economic independence their new skills brought them also brought them respect and acceptance in their families and communities. With their new found confidence as active contributors to their families, the women are no longer looked down upon.

C. Achievements

Although the project experienced some initial difficulties during its implementation period, its outcomes have made it a success story. Through the training the lives of the women trainees were expanded and enhanced. It gave the women their self-respect and confidence back, and demonstrated that they could be active members and contributors to their community and its development.

Their new found economic independence also brought social respect and acceptance. They earned this respect and acceptance in two important ways – through economic contributions to their families, and through their contributions to their community by providing much needed services and support for the rehabilitation of the physically impaired.

As importantly, the project produced a pool of female technicians – a great need identified by the earlier survey. This project will also encourage other girls and women with disabilities to take up mobility appliances to enhance their personal mobility. The project also created a new opportunity for women's vocational rehabilitation. The skills gained under the project may assist many women in the future to become economically independent if they choose to pursue the training. Furthermore, the project helped to demonstrate the potential of women with disabilities. It also showed that if well-designed training that is responsive to the needs of the local community is provided, woman with disabilities can master anything, including unconventional or male-dominated professions.

In addition to the impact on the women, the project has made an important impact on the local communities. Community attitude change has been achieved, with many families recognizing the benefits of enabling their daughters, sisters, mothers or wives to partake in skills training and enhancement.

D. Key lessons learned

This project was the first of its kind in India, and the lessons learned from its successes and failures have proved invaluable for replication and further development of the project.

One important insight provided by the project was the impact of the hidden or scarce visibility of women with disabilities. This emerged as a vital issue that needs to be addressed. In addition, further education and more accessible education need to be made available for women and girls with disabilities. The lack of a minimum education increases their vulnerability and reduces opportunities to partake in vocational and/or technical training.

It was also found that there is a lack of interest in many families in encouraging their girls and women to undertake skills training. Families often reported that they felt that women and girls with disabilities were "no good for anything", and that "their marriage prospects are very low". There is also an evident lack of interest among the women and girls themselves to take up what is often seen as an unconventional vocation. However, despite their initial lack of support and encouragement, many families took back their daughters when they started earning money as a result of their new skills.

The most important lesson learned is the impact that poverty has on women and their families. This, in addition to disability and low literacy rates, is what contributes most to the negative stereotype of women with disability as an economic burden on their families. To achieve equality, poverty as the root cause of discrimination must be tackled. By providing employment and economic opportunities through increased skill levels, RAWWD believes it was able to address this issue through its programme.

E. Sustainability

The project did not get any financial support from government. Mobility India raised funds from various other agencies. A major source of funding came from MIBLOU, Switzerland.

Figure 4. Members of RAWWD and MIBLOU representatives

After the training, Mobility India assisted the trainees to find a suitable location for setting up a workshop. A site was found just opposite one of the largest hospitals in Bangalore, and where most of the clients for fitments come from. Cheshire Home provided the space free of charge in return for free service to the children at the home with disabilities – an example of sharing resources.

In the first year, Mobility India gave full financial support to the running of the workshop, including the salary of the members. This was reduced gradually over three years until the workshop became self-sufficient. At the end of the third year, Mobility India was able to bring to a close its involvement and hand over the workshop to the trainees. Within four years of operation the women running and working in the workshop were drawing regular salaries, had set up a bank account and had accumulated considerable savings. On seeing the success of this project, other groups are voicing interest in replicating the programme.

The workshop is now run and managed entirely by the women themselves. They not only make orthotics, prosthetics, and rehabilitation devices, but also train other young women and girls in the manufacture of these aids and devices. In addition, the income generated by selling the devices ensures that they are self-sustainable – able to continue their activities, run their business, and save for the future and for further growth and income.

Mobility India continues to provide technical support when needed, and to provide training to upgrade the skills of the women technicians. RAWWD has become the strongest partner of Mobility India, a valued partner among its 27 other partners from all over India. Mobility India and its partners work together to reach out to as many people with disabilities, especially young girls and women, as possible.

PART THREE

EDUCATION

VIII. Overview of Education

The education of children and youth with disabilities remains one of the most serious challenges facing Governments in the Asian and Pacific region. Evidence from the review of national progress in the implementation of the Agenda for Action for the Asian and Pacific Decade of Disabled Persons suggests that fewer than 10 per cent of children and youth with disabilities have access to any form of education. The target of the Agenda for Action for the Asian and Pacific Decade of Disabled Persons to increase the enrolment of children and youth with disabilities to close the gap between their current level of enrolment and the net enrolment rate of non-disabled children in each respective country or area in the UNESCAP region has not been met.[4]

Education is a basic human right and all children, including children with disabilities, have a right to education. This right has been enshrined in the Universal Declaration of Human Rights, the Convention on the Rights of the Child, the World Declaration on Education for All, the Dakar Framework for Action on Education for All and the millennium development goals. The Convention on the Rights of the Child is the most widely ratified human rights treaty in the history of the United Nations and has been ratified by all countries and areas in the Asian and Pacific region. It mandates that States make primary education compulsory and available free to all children on the basis of equal opportunity, with protection from all kinds of discrimination, including discrimination on the basis of disability. It also requires that children with disabilities have access to, and receive education in, a manner conducive to the child's achieving the fullest possible social integration and individual development.

BMF links early detection, early intervention and education and requires, by means of its targets, that children with disabilities be an integral part of the population targeted by the Millennium Development Goal of ensuring that by 2015 all boys and girls will complete a full course of primary education. It further requires steps to be taken to provide measures for early detection and community-based early intervention for all infants and young children who need them, with support to their families.

From Thailand comes Anita's story. Her story expresses the difficulties faced by parents of infants and young children with disabilities, and the incredible initiative and resourcefulness shown by her mother. If early intervention services had been freely available from the time of her birth, Anita's passage through school may have been smoother. If schools were truly welcoming and inclusive, with teachers trained to teach children with a diverse range of abilities, the outcome of Anita's learning and enjoyment of school may have been different.

The case study from Samoa is an example of good practice that may serve as a model for other Pacific island countries in the subregion. Legislation was passed mandating education for all children and then systematic steps taken to ensure the achievement of successful implementation. One of the most significant aspects of this story is the care with which the survey of children was undertaken, the database developed for ongoing multisectoral use, the provision of appropriate school opportunities in the village communities where the disabled children were located and the linking of the plan to the teacher training system to ensure success and sustainability.

---

4   ESCAP, "Review of national progress in the implementation of the Agenda for Action for the Asian and Pacific Decade of Disabled Persons, 1993-2002" (E/ESCAP/APDDP/1).

IX. Special Needs Education Survey Project in Samoa

A. Nature of the problem

Samoa is a Pacific island nation with a population of approximately 162,000 people. Nearly half of the population is under the age of 18 years. Special Education and Disability services have been in existence in Samoa for over 20 years. Until recently these services have primarily been provided by NGOs in the forms of "special schools" and vocational training, and all in Apia, the capital city. Parents and the extended family have been the primary caregivers and have received little support, information or resources.

The Convention on the Rights of the Child (CRC), of which Samoa is a signatory, mandates the State to provide primary education to all on an equal basis of opportunity. It also requires that children with disabilities have access to and receive education which will assist them to achieve the fullest possible social integration and individual development. Despite this, the recognition of the Government's responsibility in caring and providing for children with disabilities is a relatively new concept in Samoa. It was not until 1991, through the *Education Amendment Act 1991-1992,* that the Government's responsibility for Special Education development was acknowledged through legislation. This Act was a key piece of legislation, and further advancing the cause of special education needs for children with disabilities were the policy documents *Education Policies and Strategies 1995-2005* which clearly outline the expected contributions by the Department of Education to this area of development.

While legislation and policy acknowledged that children with disabilities had special education needs, a major challenge in delivering on this promise was the identification of those in the target group. Lack of data on the number and prevalence of children with disabilities made it impossible to formulate policies responsive to these special needs. This lack of information was contributing to the continued neglect of the rights of children with disabilities, despite the existence of international conventions such as the CRC, or national policies, such as the *Education Policies and Strategies.* Until children were identified and information about their unmet needs obtained, these policies and others in the future could not be developed into meaningful services and supports for children with disabilities in Samoa.

In recognition of this, the Special Needs Education (SNE) Survey project was developed, with its primary aim to identify all children from the ages of 0-14 with a disability. Using a conservative estimate relating to the number of people with disability in a population, it was estimated that there were approximately 1,600 children with disabilities, or roughly 1 per cent of the population. Once they were identified the next challenge was to develop education programmes to meet their needs and develop their potential.

B. Main features of the organization

The Special Needs Education Survey was a cooperative effort between the Samoa Department of Education (DOE) and the United Nations Development Programme (UNDP).

A SNE Advisory Group had previously been established and became the focal point in assisting and advising the consultant hired to implement the Survey. The group had members from government (Education, Health, Youth), NGOs, the National University of Samoa, parents and people with disabilities. Their cooperation was crucial to the success of the project in that everyone shared ideas, networks and, when possible, resources to enable this project to be successful.

1. Aims of the Survey

The primary aim of the Survey was to identify all children with disabilities by:

- Location – educational district and village where they live
- Age
- Type and severity of disability
- Education and support needs

In addition, the Survey sought to analyse the collected data and information, make recommendations for Special Education services and raise issues for further consideration.

2. Process and methods

The process and methods included:

- Collation and review of all existing data on special needs children from previous surveys and other relevant literature
- Establishment of a clear and comprehensive definition of "special needs children"
- Development and design of a survey to obtain information

Two surveys were designed and developed. One was to be used by teachers and one was to be used by community nurses. While very similar, there were some variations in questions as they related to the roles and responsibilities of the two different groups. Both surveys were in English and Samoan.

It was agreed that a multi-pronged approach would offer the best opportunity to obtain accurate and comprehensive data. Major groups were targeted to obtain information about children with special needs, including school inspectors and teachers, pre-school teachers, community district nurses and disability NGOs.

3. Recording information

All information and data gathered were entered onto a specifically designed database now known as the Special Needs Education (SNE) Survey Database. It is the first national special needs database to record basic information about each individual child for whom information was received. The database has been designed so that it is compatible with the computer software and systems used by the Department of Education, and will be used to continuously update Department of Education information for the purposes of record keeping and planning.

4. Analysing information

All data obtained and entered in the SNE Survey Database were inspected to ensure the highest level of accuracy. The information was analysed for the following categories:

- Details for individual children

- Number, type and age range of disabilities accounted for in each school district and village

- National summaries of types and severity of disabilities

In analysing the data it must be acknowledged that the knowledge base amongst the key target groups and even within the target groups, varied considerably. While this did not affect the identification process, it is estimated that because of this variance the figures obtained in the survey must be regarded as conservative.

The survey identified and verified 991 children representing 0.6 per cent of the Samoan population.

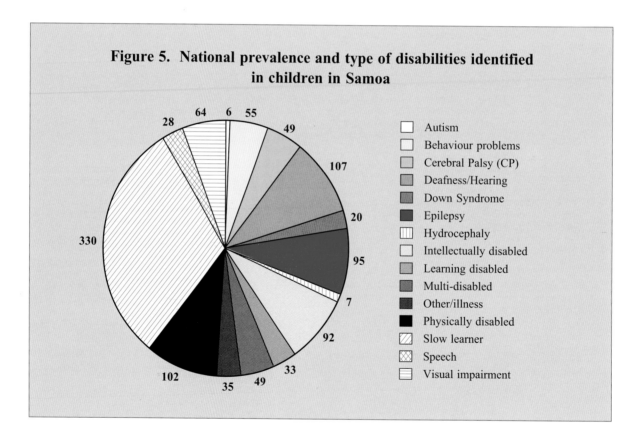

Figure 5. National prevalence and type of disabilities identified in children in Samoa

Once the data were handed over to the Department of Education, a period of evaluation and planning took place. The database format was scrutinized and some changes were made so that it could accommodate additional information. Whether a child had an Individual Education Programme (IEP) prepared for them, whether they had or needed a special aid such as a wheelchair, and records of visits made to the child and their family and progress were able to be recorded in the Comments section. The database moved from identification to programme development, but the original framework of individual, village, district, national, disability and severity was maintained.

The strength of this system of information storage is that it functions from two distinctly different positions. Firstly, it is able to provide statistical information relating to planning needs. For example, the numbers of children with hearing impairment in a particular education district. This is valuable for planning for teacher training, for allocation of travel funds etc. However, the database also gives detailed information on each of these children with hearing impairment, and their individual needs. The focus of the database is the child, their family and how best the Department of Education can meet their educational needs.

C. Achievements

In February 2001, six months after the completion of the Special Needs Education Survey, the Samoa Department of Education opened the first Special Needs Unit in a village school. It was staffed by the first Special Education teacher graduates from the National University of Samoa's Faculty of Education. This school is in an education district recommended by the consultant who carried out the survey, using the information gained. In 2002, four more Special Needs Units opened, three in rural villages; once again the decision for placement was made from the information in the database.

The raised awareness as a result of the survey also contributed to the appointment of a Special Needs Education Coordinator to the Curriculum Development Unit of the Department of Education in February 2002. Four Special Education teacher graduates also participated in a one-month intensive practical placement in New Zealand. In addition, a series of training sessions in sign language was conducted for parents of children with severe hearing problems, and teachers from each of their village schools. A series of training sessions for teachers and parents of children with visual impairment was also carried out.

Also important to note is the closer working relationship that has been established between the Departments of Education and Health. This is evident in the training sessions held for Community Health Nurses, to better equip them in early identification of children with developmental delay. The Departments are collaborating to produce a poster, pamphlet and short television documentary to help parents and teachers better understand and deal with epilepsy in children.

Perhaps the greatest achievement has been the increased enrolment of children with disabilities into regular schools. The Department of Education encourages parents to give their children this opportunity and special education staff visit schools and provide support for these children and their teachers.

All teacher trainees now undertake one Special Education paper in their training. From establishment in 1998, there are now four lecturers involved in this area at the Faculty of Education.

With the Department of Education making a major commitment to children with special needs, others have become more encouraged and committed to work in this area. The resulting change in community attitudes has contributed to the establishment of a self-advocacy group for people with disabilities. Its establishment in Apia is perhaps in part the result of a more enlightened and accepting environment regarding disability.

Finally, in July 2002, the United Nations Development Programme (UNDP) began a project entitled *Empowering Rural People with Disabilities.* The impetus for this came from the Special Needs Education Survey. The data provided by the Survey convinced planners that there was a need for support, and that such a project was in line with the Government's priorities for assistance for rural communities and poverty alleviation.

D. Lessons learned

It is important that the SNE Advisory Group continues to work together closely and to produce a long-term plan or vision. While there should always be room for the Department of Education to respond quickly to needs, it is important too to have a clear idea of what services for children with special needs will look like in five years time, and in 10.

The move to make pre-service training in Special Education compulsory has been a great step forward and is indicative of the support given by the Faculty of Education to this area of education. It is important that training in this area is incorporated into all in-service work, so that the issue becomes more inclusive, rather than a separate area of concern.

Lastly, there is no doubt that families do care about their children and want the very best for them. This includes giving their children with disabilities the opportunity to attend school just like other children. There are also many teachers who believe that these children should be part of their village school and, in spite of having no training in the area, try to integrate them into their class programmes. These teachers need to be acknowledged for their efforts and given as much support as possible.

E. Sustainability

The extremely low rate of access to education for children with disabilities is a major area for concern in the Asian and Pacific region. It remains one of the most important issues to be addressed in the coming decade. The Special Needs Education Survey has provided Samoa with hard data that can not be ignored. However, it is obvious that there is still much to be done. Although the majority of the children categorized as Slow Learners are in school, they are not as yet receiving an education that meets their special need. Children with hearing impairment are seldom able to communicate with their families and if they are in school, the signing competence of their teachers is still minimal. Children with visual impairment may have some Braille support via NGO assistance, but accessing remote villages and schools makes this difficult. In addition, while mainstream teachers are often sympathetic to the concept of including children with special needs into their village school, when faced with the reality many feel nervous and not competent.

While it is easy to feel overwhelmed by what is still to be done, it must be acknowledged that much has been achieved in the last five years. An excellent beginning has been made with the establishment of Special Education within the Department of Education. The greatest change perhaps has been in the attitudes and expectations of both those with disabilities and society in general. Many parents now expect that their children can become part of the education system. Many adults with disability now expect to work in paid employment and to continue in tertiary education. People with disabilities are now are seen on television and in public places. The move by the Education Department to include students with special learning needs into its programmes has been a demonstration of commitment noted by the whole country. It has given heart to families of disabled children and adults with disabilities and encouraged them to move forward themselves towards inclusive practices.

This process is exciting to observe and is true social action towards a more civil society. Central to this change has been the Special Needs Education Survey. No longer are the disabled hidden and faceless. Samoa has seen their faces, knows their names and now is facing the challenge of fully integrating these citizens into the mainstream of Samoan life. The Department of Education cannot do this alone, but with help and support of the whole nation it is possible.

Figure 6. Students from a special needs class and their teacher

X. Thailand: A Parent's Story

A. Nature of the problem

"**I** *was so happy on the day my daughter was born. But my happiness quickly turned to shock when I learnt that she had Downs' Syndrome. Her IQ is lower than ordinary children. Her physical development is slower too. What could I do to help her to develop her potential, both mentally and physically?"*

The words of Poranee, describing her feelings on the birth of her daughter Anita, are undoubtedly familiar to many parents of children born with a disability. Unprepared for such a difficult future, not sure where to turn to get help and uncertain of their own abilities to parent their child, many feel alone and isolated. In the 1980s, when Anita and her family first returned to Thailand, the lack of government support and services available to children with disabilities and their families was strikingly apparent compared with France where the family had been living for the first years of Anita's life.

In France, the State had provided numerous support services for children with disabilities, including physical therapy, transport, medical services and so on. But in Thailand, not only were these services not available, even more basic needs such as education were poorly served.

Education is a basic human right, and all children including those with disabilities have a right to education. Children with disabilities have the right to access and receive education in a manner conducive to achieving their fullest possible social integration and individual development. Yet in Thailand as in many countries in the Asian and Pacific region, there are a limited number of special schools, and even fewer teachers with the skills required to teach children with special needs.

Exclusion from, or inadequate, education is also a key risk factor for poverty. Inadequate education at the primary level restricts opportunities for pursuing vocational training and employment later in life, and ultimately limits the opportunities for these children to develop to their fullest potential. Failure to access education and training further prevents the achievement of economic and social independence. Children with disabilities who are denied access to an adequate education often become economic burdens on their communities and their families. Most families and communities are ill-equipped to deal with the responsibilities that come with this dependence.

B. Main features of the organization

Poranee, through her own experience, recognized how heavy this burden, when carried alone, could be. But as a parent, she knew how determined most parents are to do all that they can to help their children achieve their fullest potential. She decided to set up a support network for parents to help each other.

Poranee set up the Parent's Support Association in 1999, after attending a seminar on employment for disabled people arranged by the Council of Disability which had failed to include people with learning disabilities. Concerned at their exclusion, even by the Council of Disability, she set up the Association with the hope of providing an opportunity for parents of children with a disability to meet and to provide support to one another, and a sense of shared hope for their children.

Additionally through the Association, Poranee lobbied government agencies to provide more services and educational materials for children with disability, and approached private companies and donors with requests for financial support, or assistance making teaching toys and books she had designed, based on her own experiences teaching her daughter to read and count.

C. Achievements

1. Developing children's fullest potential

One of Poranee's greatest achievements has been the inspiration she has provided by refusing to accept the limited educational opportunities available for her daughter. Recognizing that she needed intensive education support from as early as possible, Poranee developed her own teaching tools and curriculum.

All children with learning impairment can reach their full potential if given the chance – especially if started early. Poranee took a three-step approach to parenting Anita. First, she raised her as an ordinary child, refusing to limit her hopes for her. Second, she began charting her steps of development and when Anita did not instinctively develop skills such as crawling and walking, she taught her herself. Third, she focused on developing language in Anita. She talked and played with her. She told her the name of the clothes she wore, the food she ate, objects she saw. Poranee also developed learning games for Anita such as developing memory and word and image recognition through picture cards.

Anita made great progress and at the age of three used the word "mother" for the first time. A week later she began to talk about characters in a book Poranee had been reading to her. Poranee's hard work was beginning to pay off. Anita was developing listening and comprehension skills and spoke out when she had enough confidence in herself. Then she began to form sentences and sing songs she now complete with actions. Eventually she moved to more advanced steps.

Poranee started to teach her to read when she was about six years old. She bought a set of 26 cubes. One side had a picture and the other side a letter of the alphabet. Every time she pulled out a cube, Poranee showed her the picture and told her the name. When she knew all the names, Poranee began to teach her through a similar game how to spell, using two letter words: at, on, up, etc. Gradually Anita learnt to read. Even Anita's speech therapist was surprised by her progress.

Her physical and coordination skills were also developing well. At age five she was able to ride a four-wheel cycle and at age eight, a bicycle, and then following her lead, the whole family learnt. She also learnt to swim, and at the age of eight she learnt to play table tennis. Anita's skills as a table tennis player progressed so well that she eventually competed on behalf of Thailand in table tennis at the "Special Olympic Games" in Connecticut, U.S.A.

Anita progress was very promising – she was even able to attend a local school. The most common form of education for children with intellectual handicaps, as with children with other disabilities, is in a segregated special school. Such schools are mostly located in urban areas, and have limited capacity and resources. But the best opportunity for learning for children with disabilities is in inclusive or integrated education. Access to regular local neighbourhood or community schooling provides the best opportunity for children with disabilities, including those who are intellectually handicapped. Therefore, Poranee was determined to ensure Anita was able to attend a local school. When she did, Anita loved it, enjoying being with other children and enjoying the inclusive learning environment.

Unfortunately, Anita's progress and Poranee's determined efforts suffered a major setback when an inexperienced teacher hit Anita in class for disobeying a request. The incident hurt Anita deeply. She withdrew from her friends at school, and at home became quiet and sullen. Her smiling face was replaced with an angry, dark cloud. Poranee and her husband took Anita to see a child psychologist but it took her years to recover from the blow. But Poranee's goal for Anita remains the same – to help her develop her abilities to think and reason to a level where she can obtain a degree of independence.

2. Parent support

The ill-measured response of the teacher under who's care Anita was placed, is indicative of a lack of training and understanding of the special needs of children with disabilities. The lack of skilled, experienced teachers equipped to care for children with disabilities in local schools is one of the many challenges faced by children with intellectual handicaps and their parents. Adding to this challenge is the lack of support available for parents themselves when something like this happens. Many do not know how to respond, or where to turn to get advice or support. Parenting can be a difficult, isolating, intimidating experience at the best of times. But the lack of support services for parents of children with intellectual handicaps makes it even more so.

When Anita and her family returned to Thailand there were teacher support associations but no such network or group for parents. Further, many of those working in the disability area were not parents themselves and did not understand a parent's need. There was obviously a desperate need to set up some kind of group or organization that could help parents in particular. Recognizing the need, Poranee took matters into her own hands.

Setting up the Parents' Support Association was not so difficult, but convincing parents to participate in it was. Many felt that they were already struggling to take care of themselves, without adding the burden of feeling responsible for other parents. So the first thing Poranee did was to raise awareness of the Association amongst parents and the community in general.

She asked a well-respected politician, Khunying Supatra Masdit, to talk about the Association on an in-depth news analysis programme on local television. The programme drew a large response, and calls from parents flooded in afterwards. The depth of need and isolation felt by many parents was revealed by the number who rang to make requests for personal assistance to help get their children into schools. Her main objective was to convince parents not to give up hope, and to assist them in finding ways to help develop their children's potential as much as possible. The Association has about 50 members, along with wide ranging networks with other NGOs working in the disability sector.

In addition to providing regular support group meetings, the Association conducts interventions at schools, and holds workshops with education, medical and psychological specialists invited to talk to parents to provide assistance and feedback. Through the Association parents are also able to access overseas special teaching materials, translated by the Association into Thai. With funding from the Thai Government and NGOs, Poranee has also written four books on teaching reading and writing to children with intellectual handicaps. These books are now being sent to all special and integrated schools and parents all over Thailand, free of charge.

D. Lessons learned

What has become clear from Poranee's experience with her own daughter Anita, and through her sharing of other parents' experience through the Parent Support Association, is that children with intellectual handicaps can develop greatly, and often beyond expectations, if given the right opportunities and the right support. But to do that in a developing country where there are few State funded support services, requires great energy and determination from the parents. Hence, a network such as the Parents' Support Association is vital in helping parents maintain the energy and goals for their child's development in an environment where there is little support.

E. Sustainability

Like most parents of children with disabilities, Poranee's greatest worry for Anita is what will become of her should anything happen to her. The existing centres for children with disabilities are greatly understaffed and under-resourced. Poranee, through the Parents Support Association, is hoping to build a centre for children with intellectual handicaps which will be able to provide full-time care and vocational training for children with special needs. The centre, the Saint Ann's House Project has been set up with the Sisters of the Camellias. It will have the capacity to care for up to 20 girls with intellectual handicaps, so that they can have a safe place to live like other children.

Figure 7. Poranee and Anita at the Special Olympics in Connecticut

PART FOUR

ACCESSIBILITY

XI. Overview of Accessibility

Barriers to physical environments are frequently cited as one of the most significant limitations facing persons with disabilities. Certainly they are one of the most obvious. As such, this policy area received much attention during the first Asian and Pacific Decade of Disabled Persons. In 1994, UNESCAP undertook the development of regional guidelines for the promotion of non-handicapping environments for persons with disabilities and older persons. The guidelines cover planning and building design, access policy provisions and legislation and the promotion of public awareness to improve access. The guidelines were published in 1995.

The second phase of the project was to implement the guidelines in three pilot projects. These were conducted in Bangkok, Beijing and New Delhi. Actual accessibility improvements were achieved at all three sites and the pilot projects led Governments to the examination of policies and programmes concerning accessibility for people with disabilities and the issuance of improved regulations on accessibility.

In 2000, a unique initiative was undertaken to train a group of young disabled persons as promoters of non-handicapping environments. The concept of "non-handicapping" was extended to include all kinds of barriers faced by persons with disabilities. Social mobilization and advocacy skills became a core part of the training, which was conducted in three parts over a period of one year. At their graduation in December 2000, this group formed the Access Initiative Network, one of the first networks in the region to link persons with disabilities and their non-disabled friends and partners with a dedicated focus on disability, and on access issues in particular. Many members of this group have undertaken significant projects in a variety of areas, formed their own disability-focused NGOs and have ended up in leadership roles in self-help organizations across the region.

Both case studies presented in this section are the work of graduates of the "class of 2000". The case study from Indonesia describes a project that was aimed at restoring an ancient and, historical market site, and ensuring in the process that it became accessible to persons with disabilities. This project has required persistence, a high degree of technical skill and, above all, well-honed advocacy skills. Difficulties and setbacks encountered were met with the unshakeable belief that people with disabilities have the same rights as anyone else to access their cultural heritage.

The defining characteristic of the work of Sudhakara from Hyderabad is that no barrier will remain unchallenged. Trained as an engineer, his technical skills have been well utilized as he addressed problems in roads, railways, transport, and buildings. His unswerving determination has as easily been aroused when confronting barriers to tertiary education for young people with disabilities as to more obvious physical obstacles. His advocacy has been directed at persons in the highest positions of power and his use of the media in his campaigns has been masterly. His work has received international recognition and in 2000 he was awarded a Helen Keller Award for his disability rights activism and advocacy.

XII. Creating a Barrier-free Marketplace: Pasar Gede, Central Java

A. Nature of the problem

In 2001, a Solo NGO, Talenta, in partnership with the Kakak Foundation, conducted a survey of public facilities in Solo. At the end of the three-month survey period, the survey concluded the majority of public facilities in Solo did not meet the accessibility needs of people with disabilities. That was despite a Decree by the Minister of Public Works (468/KPTS/1998) on Technical Requirements on Accessibility for Public Spaces and Buildings and former President, Abdulrahman Wahid, establishing the National Accessibility Movement in 2000.

In the developing world in particular, questions about accessibility to public buildings and services are often overlooked because of concerns over cost, or because of lack of expertise. But with the Pasar Gede marketplace, a unique opportunity existed to create a barrier-free environment for all, by raising concerns over accessibility at the most crucial stage – the planning stage.

Pasar Gede Harjonagoro, one of the main traditional markets in Surakarta, was built in the royal governance period of Sri Susuhunan Pakubuwono X (1839-1939). Along with the historical importance of the marketplace, the building itself also has historical value, as it was built by famous Dutch architect, Thomas Karsten, during the Dutch colonialization of Indonesia.

Pasar Gede was renovated for the first time during 1927-1930. At that time the site area was enlarged to over 200 square metres, resulting in the building being expanded to two-stories. In 1947, the market was renovated again, after it was seriously damaged during a riot between the Indonesians and the Dutch colonialists. Restoration was undertaken two years later. Then later, between 1986 and 1987, a further development took place and two new buildings were added at the west side of the main building. These buildings remained in place until a fire broke out in the market early one morning in April 2000.

The Pasar Gede was significantly damaged during the fire, the cause of which was alleged to have been electrical failure. Pasar Gede was rebuilt a year later. But the restoration became the subject of great division, with many groups, individuals and organizations fighting for their own interests and advantages, and little interest being paid to the concerns or rights of people with disability who wished to access the marketplace.

Talenta launched a campaign to include the issue of accessibility for people with disability into the rebuilding brief of the architects, but the idea of "universal design" or equality of access for all faced several challenges. These included:

- Lack of understanding and awareness of the equal rights of all people, whether able bodied or not

- Lack of knowledge, expertise or support for universal design or barrier-free environment

- Lack of existing examples for local communities to learn about barrier-free environments, especially in public places

The concept of "universal design" did not have universal understanding prior to Talenta's campaign.

B. Main features of the organization

Talenta is a non-governmental organization focused on the promotion of non-handicapping or barrier-free environments. As such, Talenta took part in public discussions held by the local government and other organizations concerned with the redesign and rebuilding of Pasar Gede.

Talenta has extensive networks with many city stakeholders and other organizations, groups or individuals involved in, or advocating for, increasing and increased accessibility and equal right of access for all. These include the Accessibility Study Group (Architecture Department of Sebelas Maret University), KOMPAGG (Traders of Pasar Gede Community) and LAB-UCYD (Laboratory of Urban Crisis and Community Development of Sebelas Maret University) and other NGOs in Solo. Through this network, a concerted campaign was undertaken to raise awareness of the concept of a barrier-free environment and inclusion of the concept in the redesign of Pasar Gede.

Through the campaign, it was proposed that the rebuilding of Pasar Gede be in keeping as much as possible with the marketplace's original design, with the Indiesch building style maintained, whilst ensuring the market became a barrier-free environment.

It was also hoped that by strong involvement of a network of groups concerned with accessibility, should problems in accessibility be identified, such as traffic and parking, lobbying for improvements on the design (including building and the surrounding area) could be successfully made. Further, it was hoped that inclusion of some basic principles of universal design/barrier-free environment in the new design would be made, such as:

- Accessible toilets/lavatories

- Identifiable path for the blind on the pavement/sidewalk (guiding blocks and warning blocks)

- Accessible ramps

- International sign of accessibility at two main entrances

C. Achievements

Pasar Gede now has been completed with ramps, accessible toilets/lavatories, and a pedestrian path with guiding and warning blocks for the blind. There are also multilingual signs advising of accessibility at two main entrances. Pasar Gede has become a demonstration project in combining the goals of accessibility and cultural preservation, with its traditional marketplace redesign.

As a result of the strong advocacy and technical support of Talenta, the building has been preserved both in character and usage. It maintained the key elements of a traditional market with Indiesch building style. Most importantly, it has been able to combine these elements with the principles of universal design, achieving a barrier-free environment.

Figure 8. Side railings and sloping paths inside Pasar Gede

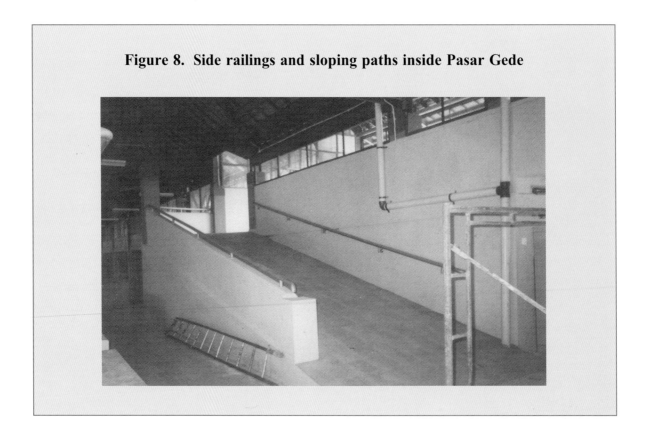

The strong advocacy work of Talenta, which included representations to local government officials, attending public meetings on the redesign of the marketplace, and even conducting public meetings of its own, was responsible for bringing about a change in attitudes amongst its partners in government. One example of such change was the promise that a local law will be drawn up to oversee the implementation of accessibility in public spaces and buildings in Solo. In addition, the Ministry of Public Works announced it would assist in enforcing the Decree on Technical Requirements on Accessibility for Public Spaces and Buildings. The Ministry embraced its responsibility to ensure universal design and equality of access for all, and now describes its role as the "building police", responsible for ensuring new buildings meet all accessibility requirements. Increased policy and legislative support for the goal of a barrier-free environment is another promising outcome of Talenta's determined advocacy efforts.

The achievements of Talenta in ensuring that Pasar Gede is accessible to all are considerable. It now serves as a living example of what can be achieved by the combined efforts of advocacy and public awareness raising. In addition, it has helped heal some of the wounds of more turbulent and violent times, serving also as a symbol of reconciliation and community participation in Solo.

D. Key lessons learned

Key lessons learned from the redevelopment of Pasar Gede include the recognition that:

- The building development process should be supervised intensively to avoid differences between planning and implementation.

- Advocacy, networking and intensive public campaigning is extremely important in raising understanding and awareness, not only of universal design, but also of the concept of equal rights for all.

- The public awareness campaign was important not just in raising awareness about accessibility and the rights of people with disabilities, but also in bringing together city stakeholders such as the local government, architects, urban planners, the university, NGOs, people with disabilities, community leaders, mass media and legislative bodies to understand the barrier-free environment and society.

E. Sustainability

In order to ensure sustainability of the gains of Pasar Gede in terms of creating accessible and barrier-free environments in Indonesia, an intensive campaign about the success of the barrier-free environment designed for Pasar Gede will be conducted. It is hoped this will increase awareness, as well as usage, of the barrier-free environment of Pasar Gede. It is further hoped that through this increased awareness, understanding and support for the concept of accessibility as a right will be developed.

In the future, evaluations of the barrier-free facilities in Pasar Gede will be undertaken to identify any problems such as maintenance and socialization of barrier-free facilities that may emerge.

More generally, in terms of universal design in public places, Talenta aims to:

- Make more barrier-free environments in public places such as schools, campuses, and offices.

- Use lessons that have been learned from Pasar Gede to assist in the better implementation of universal design.

- Implement universal design not just in public but also private places such as homes.

- Conduct a public awareness campaign including information, knowledge, attitudes, law enforcement and models of universal design concepts which must be spread to as many stakeholders as possible.

- Continue to coordinate and collaborate with stakeholders such as the local government, architects, urban planners, engineers, universities, NGOs, people with disabilities, community leaders, mass media and legislative bodies to establish and strengthen access-related networking.

In terms of the design process, architects should engage in discussion and consultation with people with disabilities themselves who could act as resource persons. Architects and planners should also be aware and knowledgeable of accessibility and barrier-free environment issues and universal design. Talenta plans to take immediate action to promote the inclusion of barrier-free environment design in the curricula for the training of architects, engineers, and urban and rural planners as well as in the Architecture Department of universities.

Finally, Talenta aims to pressure the local government to pass the Regulation Law concerning the standard and implementation of barrier-free environments. An access officer is being appointed by the local authority (Urban Planning of the City Government) to check thoroughly that drawings do comply.

XIII. An Advocate in India: Sudhakara P. Reddy

A. Nature of the problem

Hyderabad is the fifth largest city in south India, and one of its fastest growing. At present the main modes of public transportation in the city are overcrowded buses, three-wheeled taxis and manual rickshaws. Bicycles and motorized two-wheelers are the most popular personal transportation.

Accessibility for people with disabilities in the city is extremely poor. So too unfortunately is public awareness of the problem. Few, if any, of the State-owned railway or bus terminals have access elements such as ramps, railings, or grip bars in toilets. This is despite the passing of the Persons with Disabilities Act, 1995 which mandates certain provisions of accessible public transportation. Furthermore, there are no design guidelines and the awareness among public transport officials of access issues and barrier-free environments is very low.

The lack of accessibility in Hyderabad was highlighted by a tragic railway accident in 2001 that resulted in the death of three visually impaired women and the injury of 11 others when they were struck down by a local train as they were trying to cross the railway tracks. The South Central Railway (SCR) described the accident as an "unusual occurrence of trespassing over railway tracks leading to the death and injuries to passenger".[5] But at same time the SCR had failed to implement the Central Public Works Department (CPWD) guidelines on provision of barrier-free environments to people with disability by providing safe crossing alternatives for people with disabilities.

The lack of accessibility of railway terminals in Hyderabad was the real cause of the accident. This is just one example of the challenge and the real physical threat posed to people with disabilities by environments that are not sensitive to their needs. In this particular case though, the tragedy provided the spur for direct action by Sudharkara P. Reddy and the advocacy group founded by him – Society for Equal Opportunities for Persons with Disabilities (Se'DOP). They took the issue to the press and demanded that the issue of accessibility of public transportation be raised as an issue for all in the community.

B. Main features of the organization

Sudharkara P. Reddy describes himself as both a disability rights activist and a research professional working on the development of high technology products. As a disability rights campaigner, his aim has been to build awareness of disability issues from a rights-based perspective, as well as focusing on policy advocacy. Sudharkara is deeply committed to improving the situation of disabled persons. He has actively advocated for the rights of people with disability in the areas of education, accessibility of public places and accessible public transportation, and for effective implementation of the Persons with Disabilities Act in Andhra Pradesh.

---

5 *Deccan Chronicle,* 25th April 2001.

Suffering from a severe form of muscular dystrophy, and using a wheelchair, it is his own personal experience that gives Sudharkara his vision, and his commitment that gives him strength. He has been instrumental in bringing to public attention many key issues for those in the disability sector, emphasizing the rights-based approach. He has done this in large part through the Society for Equal Opportunities for Persons with Disabilities (Se'DOP).

Founded by Sudharkara in January 1999, Se'DOP is an advocacy group dedicated to securing equal opportunities, full participation and protection of the rights of persons with disabilities. Se'DOP is committed to eliminating all barriers that prevent persons with disabilities from enjoying full equality. Se'DOP is primarily of, and directed by, persons with disability. It is one of the few, if not the only, policy advocacy group in the State of Andhra Pradesh, India.

The organization's main focus is on improving educational facilities for the disabled. However, one of the most important features of Se'DOP's activities is not the specific issue they may focus on, but their energy and commitment in rousing public support to pressure their government representatives to meet their responsibilities in providing equal access for all.

C. Achievements

Main achievements have been in raising the issue of access and public transportation for people with disabilities in both the media and in the wider community. Se'DOP and its founder, with great determination and expertise, have tirelessly advocated on the behalf of people with disability, and most importantly, with considerable success.

1. Making public transport more accessible

One of Se'DOP's most important and successful campaigns undertaken was the campaign to ensure the new Multimodal Suburban Commuters Transportation System (MSCT) being designed for the Hyderabad urban area was barrier-free for people with disability. Given the size and scope of the system, this was no small undertaking. Se'DOP began by raising concerns over general accessibility in the design plans for the MSCT through Office of the Chief Commissioner for Persons with Disabilities (CCPD). The Office is the highest statutory authority charged with protecting the rights of disabled persons under the Persons with Disability Act (1995).

Se'DOP made 13 separate submissions and representations to the Chief Commissioner's Office over a period of 10 months, from November 2000 to September 2001. The submissions continually brought to the awareness of the Chief Commissioner the barriers encountered by persons with diverse disabilities at railway stations, coaches and surrounding areas. Furthermore, the submissions challenged the CCPD to direct the concerned implementing agencies to incorporate accessible design features throughout the mobility chain to make the MSCT a truly accessible public transportation system.

Eventually, 14 months of submissions and rejoinders culminated in a hearing with the CCPD, wherein the Executive Director (Perspective Planning), Railway Board, Director (Land and Amenities), Deputy Chief Engineer, South Central Railway all personally appeared before the Chief Commissioner for Persons with Disabilities and gave their commitment to ensuring all new stations built by the project would be equally accessible to all. Further, they agreed that all existing stations would be retrofitted in a phased manner. The commitment was formalized in a Government Order, the operating section of which states that:

"The Government, after careful examination, hereby directs that all Government Departments, Local Authorities, and Agencies shall provide barrier-free environments in all new buildings and public utilities for easy access of persons with disabilities with immediate effect."

The impact of Se'DOP's advocacy and lobbying cannot be underestimated. Their determined efforts ensured that the MSCT will be accessible for all. They also raised the issue of accessible public transportation within state government agencies and with legislators in Hyderabad. The state government has even written to the Ministry of Railway of the Government of India, as 50 per cent partners in the MSCT, to initiate action to meet Se'DOP's accessibility goals. Se'DOP and Sudharkara's success serves as an inspiring example and challenge to all working towards the goal of accessibility and a barrier-free environment.

To ensure accessibility remains on the agenda, Se'DOP initiated training of grass-roots campaigners on issues of accessibility to public places and public transport. The available literature was translated into the local language and circulated. Se'DOP has also provided inputs to workshops and training materials on accessible public transport at a national level.

2. Generating awareness and changing attitudes

Growing awareness of access as an issue for the whole community has perhaps been the greatest success of Sudhakara and Se'DOP. They have obtained this by strategic and savvy use of the media to reach the community, community leaders, representatives and decision-makers. Particularly satisfying has been the raised awareness and subsequent commitments gained in areas of government, legislature and justice not directly connected to social or disability welfare. One such example of this was the admission by the chairman of the Andra Pradesh Judicial Academy that there was poor disability awareness amongst judicial officers. He made this admission following attendance at a training workshop on disability and the law organized by Se'DOP in partnership with the Human Rights Law Network, and the National Centre for Promotion of Employment for Disabled People. Following the chairman's admission he pledged to include disability awareness training in the training programmes of Judicial Officers at his Academy.

Another successful campaign to change attitudes followed Se'DOP's building audit of a newly completed, prestigious public university. The building failed to meet accessibility requirements, so Se'DOP turned to the media to pressure the government and the building's architects to make changes. One important outcome of this was that through the media, the professional standards of architects who failed to meet accessibility requirements were questioned, perhaps for the first time. The media charged the building with being a "wastage of public money" and talked of "blacklisting architects for not discharging their professional responsibility". As a result the dynamics of the debate over public accessibility was expanded to include for the first time the issue of responsibility of builders and architects (in addition to their government partners) to provide non-handicapping environments.

3. Public recognition

There have been many achievements of Se'DOP and its founder Mr. Sudhakara P. Reddy. Recognition of this was given in 2002 when Sudhakara received a State Government Award for Outstanding Contribution to the Creation of a Barrier-free Environment. This award in and of itself is an achievement, as it was revived after a gap of 10 years in the giving of the Award, as a result of advocacy by Se'DOP.

In 2003 Sudhakara was recipient of the NCPEDP Helen Keller Award. Sudhakara was awarded for his individual contribution as a person with disability who has been active as an ambassador for the employment of disabled people and as a positive role model for others.

D. Lessons learned

"It is only the crying child who gets picked up"

Strong advocacy work is needed to influence people to make changes and advocacy can not work without the support of the mass media. The media have a tremendous influence in shaping public attitudes and beliefs. Non-disabled people have limited understanding of disability issues, and the media often perpetuate the problem rather than addressing it. The media in democratic countries play an important public service role by providing a platform for advocacy and for awareness raising. Non-mainstream groups and their needs and challenges will remain invisible unless they are able to use the media to raise awareness and then use this awareness to pressure their governments into responding to and addressing their needs and rights. When the media take note, opinion makers take note, and they in turn influence communities and policy and decision makers. Therefore, effective use of the media, and in turn sensitive reportage, can lead not just to increased awareness but to community attitude change, and ultimately to policy change.

E. Sustainability

"Awareness is the buzz word"

According to an article published in the Deccan Chronicle,[6] "The Society for Equal Opportunities for Persons with Disability (Se'DOP) at Gandhinagar is one such rare organization which advocates for the rights of the disabled. The volunteers of this organization believe that change can be brought about only when the physically challenged, too, become a part of the mainstream".

If people with disabilities are to become part of the mainstream, and once there maintain their position within the mainstream, issues which concern them need to have a strong and constant presence in the media. Perhaps most importantly, to sustain change, the next generation must be enlisted. All those who are entrusted with responsibility for our children – teachers, parents, etc., have a responsibility to help build a more inclusive society. More than 60 million Indians live with some kind of disability; more than 10 million are children. By starting with children, the next generation, it is possible to build not just a more accessible country but a more inclusive one.

---

[6] Ibid.

PART FIVE

EMERGING TRENDS: INFORMATION AND COMMUNICATION TECHNOLOGY

XIV. Overview of Information and Communication Technology

Information and communication technology (ICT) is now regarded as indispensable for public, business, and personal productivity and improvement of livelihoods. In the last several years, there has been much progress in the world in ICT development. This has opened up many opportunities for people with disabilities, especially in networking, solidarity, employment and independent living. Assistive computer technology and other augmentative communication products make for easy access to information and communication for people with disabilities. However, people with disabilities in the Asian and Pacific region still face multiple barriers in accessing ICT and the skills and knowledge required to benefit from it.

The transformation of the Internet from a text-based medium to a multimedia environment is also resulting in difficulties for people with visual disabilities. With a text-based medium, people with visual disabilities could use a paper-less Braille keyboard to access the Internet. However, the predominantly graphical web-pages that characterize current Internet traffic pose a new challenge.

In 2003, UNESCAP initiated a new venture to disseminate web-based information with a fully accessible non-graphic web-page for blind users. In addition, documentation is distributed by CD-ROM, which is non-graphic and accessible for alternative output devices such as a speech synthesizer or paperless Braille (Braille keyboard/terminal).

Emerging as an issue of importance during the latter part of the first Asian and Pacific Decade of Disabled Persons, the BMF has identified access to information and communications, including information, communication and assistive technologies, as one of the seven priority areas for action during the next 10-year period from 2003 to 2012. The targets of the BMF in this area require that persons with disabilities should have at least the same rate of access to the Internet and related services as the other citizens in their country. It also strongly recommends that international organizations should incorporate accessibility standards for persons with disabilities in their inter-national ICT standards and Governments should adopt ICT accessibility guidelines for persons with disabilities in their national ICT policies.

The case studies in this section indicate the serious attention that is being placed on developing the means to make information fully accessible to persons with disabilities, as described in the story of 'DAISY'. Particular emphasis is placed on accessibility for students with disabilities as they pursue higher education. The partnership between the international ICT company INTEL and the National Association for the Blind in India is an indication of the way forward. With initiatives such as these, the fear that persons with disabilities will remain on the wrong side of the digital divide will be unjustified. These are exciting initiatives in a vitally important and rapidly emerging area.

XV. Equal Access for Equal Participation: The Daisy Talking Book Production Initiative

A. Nature of the problem

Over the Decade, the term "Information and Communication Technology" (ICT) has become increasingly important in most, if not all, aspects of everyday life and work. This new ICT environment, while making life easier in many ways, also requires the user to learn and adapt to its many and evolving features. In more recent times, changes in ICT and multimedia platforms have seen it transformed from a largely text-based medium to a multimedia environment. This is causing problems for people with disabilities. But the right of people with disabilities to pursue and maintain productive employment means that ways must be pursued to ensure ICT access keeps pace with its rapid technological development.

Previously, the use of ICT to create or promote employment of persons with disabilities in Thailand has taken two main approaches:

(1) Matching the physical ability of persons with disabilities with existing ICT without any modification or adaptation of the technology itself. This practice has opened up employment opportunity for individuals who can use existing technology, but has done little to move towards greater ICT accessibility for persons with disabilities;

(2) Creating and/or promoting new employment opportunities for persons with disabilities by combining skills training in ICT and accessible ICT. The practice has been limited by the high cost of imported ICT hardware and/or software produced to be accessible or added on to existing ICT to make it more accessible, the cost of making ICT accessible in the local (Thai) language, and difficulties convincing the public and government officials that ICT accessibility for persons with disabilities is a right and brings benefits to all.

It is important therefore, that the benefits of accessibility be made evident to government and communities. Making ICT more accessible can bridge the so called "digital divide" between those with access and those without. Even more inspiring, it can also bridge the information gap between people with different types of disabilities. Well developed, accessible ICT is capable of presenting information through simultaneous and synchronized multimedia for persons with varying types of disabilities and abilities. A good example of how this is possible, and the potential this creates for people with disabilities and the communities their live and work in, is DAISY – the Digital Accessible Information System.

The Digital Audio-based Information System was originally developed as digital talking book technology. It has since been expanded to the level of a completely synchronized multimedia information system. DAISY is the next generation in digital talking books. Its potential to bridge the information gap between the blind/print disabled and people at large is being increasingly recognized. Still to be addressed, however, is the extent to which blind people, as consumers of such technology, are able to access either free or commercially available DAISY production/ playback software programmes, such as SigtunaDAR, or LpStudio/Pro.

Until as little as five years ago, DAISY was unknown in Thailand. Although education for the visually impaired in Thailand has been in existence since 1939, only about 1 per cent of blind children attend school, and fewer than 200 blind students have obtained university level education. In Thailand, most of the schools or centres which provide educational or training services to the visually impaired are run by private organizations. Development and availability of teaching resources is also limited, with each school having to establish and maintain its own material production unit which serves its students only. Currently there is no library service at the national level run by the Government for the blind and those with difficulty in reading print text.

The DAISY Talking book Production Initiative in Thailand is an attempt to bring both service providers and consumers together to bring about positive changes in the area of ICT accessibility for persons with disabilities in Thailand.

B. Main features of the organization

The DAISY Talking Book Production Initiative in Thailand was set up in 1999, and is overseen by the Thailand National Committee on DAISY Production and Services (TNCD), which is an alliance of six organizations of and for blind people in Thailand. Project partners are Ratchasuda College, Mahidol University, Thailand Association of the Blind (TAB), Christian Foundation for the Blind (CFBT), Foundation for the Promotion of Employment of the Blind (FEPB), Caulfield Library for the Blind, and the Ministry of Education.

In order to facilitate the work of the committee to its fullest, Ratchasuda College, as one of the leading academic institutions for people with disabilities, was chosen to serve as the coordinating organization, taking the role of the secretariat and serving as the research, training and consulting body for other partner organizations.

The fundamental objectives of the initiative are to:

(1) Obtain and allocate necessary hardware and software for DAISY Talking Book production at each partner organization;

(2) Introduce new and innovative ICT to blind people, including professionals, experts and all agencies related to blindness in Thailand through training workshops on DAISY Talking Book production, seminars and demonstrations and ongoing technological development;

(3) Conduct both short- and long-term research and development activities to set standards for future Talking Book productions in Thailand;

(4) Identify appropriate ways of obtaining and distributing DAISY hardware and software units to end-users in Thailand, particularly those who may not be able to afford them; and

(5) Promote public awareness of blind people's fundamental rights to information access.

As part of the project, an Asia-Pacific Regional Workshop on DAISY Talking Book Production was held in Bangkok, 25-27 September 1999. The workshop was held during the first ever General Assembly of the World Blind Union in the Asia-Pacific region. This workshop was an opportunity to share the Thai initiative with other groups and organizations working with the blind in the region.

A number of training workshops were also held. The first training workshop on DAISY book production using the Sigtuna software programme was conducted at Ratchasuda College. Each member organization was able to send at least one representative to attend the workshop with funding support from the Overbrook and Nippon Network of Educational Technology for Blind and Visually Impaired People (ON-NET). At the end of the workshops, each member organization was given a copy of Sigtuna Digital Audio Recorder version 2.017 and a set of microcomputers with necessary additional hardware/software for DAISY production. Three additional sets were allocated at Ratchasuda College for research and training purposes.

A DAISY working group was also set up at Ratchasuda College. Its tasks are:

(1) Translating and preparing DAISY training material in Thai;

(2) Producing DAISY books in Thai (mainly for research purposes); and

(3) Conducting research and development activities.

C. Achievements

Since the beginning of the project there has been much progress and many achievements. More than 100 DAISY book titles have been completed. Research and development activities are in progress and blind persons are themselves involved in many of these activities. Through the use of JAWS script, they can access at least 80 per cent of Sigtuna software, and, therefore can participate in the process of DAISY production, especially in the area of sound editing and even software training. Awareness of DAISY technology amongst government officials and the public has increased and, with it, so has understanding of the rights of blind and print disabled people to equal information access. In addition, the Educational Technology Center, Ministry of Education, is planning to expand its recording studio to enable increased and improved talking book production. Moreover, the Thailand Association of the Blind (TAB) is expanding its talking book library, and changing its name to "The National Library for the Blind and Print Disabled". At least five DAISY production units will be allocated to the new library.

The project has also been able to gain the support of Her Royal Highness, Princess Maha Chakri Sirindhorn. After receiving a brief summary report, Her Royal Highness kindly granted permission for TNCD to visit her and give a presentation on DAISY technology. The presentation was very well received and has brought several positive outcomes including funds to purchase 30 PlexTalk units. These units will be allocated to 15 schools and educational centres for the blind in Thailand. This will increase by three-fold the number of playback units available in Thailand.

D. Key lessons learned

Despite the progress mentioned above, there are still many problems to face in both Thailand and elsewhere. Key challenges include:

(1) DAISY technology, both related hardware and software, for production or reading purposes, is not widely available.

(2) The right of persons with disabilities to equal information access is not as widely recognized or understood as the right to equal physical access.

(3) Blind people, especially those with good computer skills, have not been drawn upon enough or their skills acknowledged suitably, as resources for the promotion and improvement of DAISY technology.

In many countries, policies and measures to protect the workplace rights of persons with disabilities from losing their jobs, are greatly needed. In Thailand, a great number of the blind and other people with disabilities sell lottery tickets on the street as their main source of income. In 1999, plans were floated to automate the process of ticket selling, which would have seen many ticket sellers and blind people out of work. In order to protect this sector of employment, the Thailand Association of the Blind (TAB) launched a strong and effective campaign to protect the employment of the blind ticket sellers. Instead of conducting a more traditional campaign through mass rallies and public meetings, TAB decided to engage in "internet and telecommunication warfare".

Before beginning the campaign, TAB circulated its press release to various news agencies, internet mailing lists, human rights organizations and organizations of blind people around the world. In addition, constant updates on the campaign were released by the campaign organizers using a Braille note taker. The updated messages were then dictated via a mobile phone to another blind person at the national headquarters who then disseminated the latest campaign news around the world via the Internet.

The result of such an innovative campaign was beyond expectations. Many messages of support and encouragement were received, both through regular post and e-mail. There was news coverage by major news agencies, such as the BBC, AP, and Reuters. Most of all, there was strong support from the local community who appreciated the less intrusive approach of the campaign, which stayed off the streets but was still in the minds of newspaper readers and television viewers. One of the most exciting developments was that blind hackers around the world assisted the campaign by generating thousands of messages to government websites. This did not destroy data or systems but did paralyse them, replicating the frustrations experienced daily by many blind users of less accessible ICT.

After a week of campaign activities, the Government decided not to pursue its planned policy to install automatic lottery ticket machines. The "war" was won, and the jobs of many were protected. The key to this experience is that ICT can be used not just to create employment opportunities for blind people, but also to protect them. Perhaps most importantly, ICT can play an important role in generating awareness and support for the rights of people with disabilities.

E. Sustainability

Sustainability requires innovative practice for the future and universal recognition of *Equal Access for Equal Participation*. Access to ICT has the potential to transform the lives of people with disabilities. But to ensure this potential is developed in ICT as well as among users, there is a need to make certain adequate enforcement mechanisms and compliance incentives are in place to encourage governments to develop and implement legislation and standards on accessible environments.

As recognition of DAISY as a viable tool to information access for persons with disabilities is increasing, more needs to be done to guarantee that its intended primary users, blind people, are allowed not just to benefit from its development, but also have a key role in its development. ICT access for persons with disabilities is good for all. ICT can assist in promoting, creating, enhancing and protecting employment as well as impacting on all other aspects of daily life. However, for full benefits to be achieved and sustained from the promise of ICT, full and fair participation of persons with disabilities in all aspects and at levels of ICT development, design and usaged must be ensured.

The greatest force for positive change for humanity and society comes from within – this "within" means within all of us.

XVI. Placing the Blind on the Right Side of the Digital Divide

A. Nature of the problem

Access to information is a major concern area for persons with sensory impairment such as vision or hearing impairment. Until now, the primary mode of accessing information has been through print – a medium inaccessible for persons with vision impairment. Traditionally for the visually impaired there have been two alternatives to deal with this problem – Braille and/or talking books. Materials in both these media have to be specially prepared. Thus, the materials available in these media are extremely limited and, in the less developed countries of the world, virtually non-existent.

The advent and use of ICT, however, as a medium for creation, dissemination and accessing information brought about a revolution. ICT and its tools are highly flexible and provide great scope for usage by persons with vision impairment. Information available to the seeing world is now available in its entirety to the persons with vision impairment.

Globally, the educational and vocational environment went through a sea change in the 1990s. The age of the digital divide had come about. Persons who could use computers had a certain added advantage over others. It became necessary to be computer literate to obtain gainful employment.

The technology developed has revolutionized the lives of people with vision impairment in the developed world. In developing countries, the situation was less encouraging. The cost of this technology remains high. Availability of hardware and software is also limited. While persons with vision impairment in developing countries had heard about the wonders of this new technology, only a very few, more privileged, had access to either the tools or the training to make the most of this IT revolution.

Not only is ICT expensive for the individual, there is little government support given to make it more accessible to people with disabilities. In developing countries, only about 5 per cent of the blind are able to take up or access primary education. Therefore, the priority of many governments in developing countries has been on providing basic education to persons with vision impairment. Providing expensive ICT technology to the few with the skills to use it, or making existing technology more accessible at great cost, does not make good economic sense. Despite this, placing the persons with blindness on the right side of the digital divide is an important priority, and one that will in the long run enhance their chances of economic independence and provide benefits to their communities and to national development.

B. Main features of the organization

The New Delhi office of the National Association for the Blind (NAB) took up the challenge of providing accessible and affordable ICT to blind users by establishing a computer training and technology centre.

The unit started in 1993, after NAB participated as field tester in two research and development projects aimed at developing an accessible computerized information system for blind persons.

These projects were:

- *BARC (Bhabha Atomic Research Centre) speech system:* This system allowed inputs into a computer using a special six-key keyboard which enabled blind persons to type Braille codes. It had speech output, which was possible when combined with a special word processing package, which was a part of this package.

- *Computer Assistance for the Blind (CAB):* Developed by the Indian Institute of Science (IISc), Bangalore, this system used an external speech synthesizer in conjunction with screen reading software. This system added speech output to general purpose application programmes.

When NAB first took part in this training project, it was thought that a blind person would use a computer just for word processing activities. But as a result of participating in these trials, regular computer training was started at NAB using the system developed by IISc. Since then, the computer unit of NAB has undertaken various related activities to harness the potential of this revolutionary technology, including developing a special one-year foundation course for the blind.

NAB began collaborated with the Department of Electronics in 1994 to explore the possibilities of developing a curriculum for the one-year foundation course. The Department of Electronics is a government education board which sets the syllabus for computer education programmes and oversees exams for the students of institutes which are accredited by the board. NAB was granted this accreditation in 1995. As the majority of students with vision impairment in India take up humanities rather than sciences, most did not have the pre-requisites required to pursue computer programming as a profession. Therefore, the objective of the one-year training programme was to lay the foundation for a career in computer programming. Through the course, not only did students have the opportunity to enhance their employment potential, it was also realized that at a more elementary level computers are very effective as a tool for reading and writing. Computers have the potential to enable a person with vision impairment to be independent in his educational, vocational, recreational and day-to-day activities, no matter which profession he or she chooses.

As the needs of potential students of the course varied, alternate short-term training modules were also developed. Training modules differing in duration, contents covered, courseware and so on, were designed in accordance with the needs of the different categories which included:

(a) Children attending mainstream schools with a majority of students with vision who had computer studies as a subject.

(b) Children or young adults who wanted to use computers as a tool for reading and writing for continuation of education at schools and universities for academic and professional courses.

(c) Youth looking for employment on the basis of computer operation skills.

(d) Persons who were already employed in the government or private sector and wished to take computer training to keep pace with the computerization of their workplace.

(e) Persons whose vision was impaired due to age and wished to continue reading for recreational or professional purposes.

Each of these categories had different requirements. The content and accessibility requirements differed both in terms of equipment and class times and locations. Classes were put on after office hours on a weekly basis, in addition to normal classes held on a daily basis during working hours. A distance training module was also developed.

Another important feature of the training at NAB was that it was a special computer training institute which provided only training which was already in existing mainstream computer training programmes. It was decided to provide preparatory training to the vision impaired persons to ready them to graduate to mainstream professional courses and training programmes. It was considered better to be awarded a degree in computer programming from a well-reputed open computer training institute than a special training programme for the blind.

The use of computers as assistive technology is not just opening up opportunities for employment in the IT sector. It has made it possible for blind students to study accountancy, mathematics, etc. In 2000, the efforts of NAB received a major boost when it entering into a collaboration with INTEL. Prior to the collaboration, Intel was already running an innovative global computer education programme with several partners. However, this initiative with NAB was unique as for the first time the target group was persons with disability. The features of the initiative undertaken at the NAB-INTEL Computer Training and Technology centre are listed below.

1. Training

In all societies, the incidence of disability and poverty has a strong correlation. Therefore, the training offered at NAB is totally free of cost. In addition, outstation students are given free board and lodging in a hostel provided by the Centre.

To ensure sustainability of the learning and enhanced community-based capacity developed through the course, special emphasis is given to including trainees who have the potential to become trainers themselves back in their own communities. Special training modules are also designed to provide in-depth knowledge about assistive technology such as screen reading. Software is also provided to the prospective trainers and other organizations who are otherwise already trained in the use of the computer.

2. Customized and sharing resources

The books and training materials used in the course are freely downloadable. It was essential to develop special courseware which could be used through keyboard application and was based on audio clues provided by the screen reading software. The courseware is produced in Braille, audio, large print and electronic text formats to cater to the needs of persons with vision impairment.

In order to provide support to other organizations which provide computer training, NAB provides courseware at the cost of paper and printing. E-copy versions are provided free of charge to non-profit organizations providing computer training to blind persons.

3. Locally applicable, affordable technology

An important role of the Technology Unit is to ensure local, affordable technology. The NAB-INTEL Computer Technology Training Centre has undertaken and/or supported several research and development projects for the development of specific software and hardware applicable to the Indian situation. This includes developing Braille transcription software in Hindi. Previously, Braille transcription software was available for English text only. NAB developed Braille transcription software for Hindi language, which has resulted in easy production of books in Indian languages in Braille format.

NAB has also assisted in the development of a Hindi language text and speech engine with the Speech Lab at the Central Electrical and Engineering Research Institute (CEERI). Before the collaborative efforts of NAB and CEERI, there was no comprehensive Text To Speech (TTS) software for any Indian language. NAB together with CEERI, developed TTS for Hindi which is compatible with screen reading software.

In addition to the lack of locally applicable software, the cost of assistive computer technology is perhaps the single, biggest hurdle needed to be overcome by persons with blindness or low-vision. The high cost of this technology is a barrier to accessibility – as is the case for the new digital talking books. The talking books themselves are easy and cost effective to produce and distribute. The problem is the cost of purchasing the digital talking book player. The players are too expensive not just for many individuals but also many organizations and training institutions. To overcome this barrier, the NAB Technology Unit in collaboration with Indian Institute of Technology (IIT) developed a low-cost digital talking book player (DAISY). The DAISY system provides excellent navigation and random access features not available in the analogue talking books, and is set to become the next generation in digital talking books. Now the new, low-cost version developed by NAB and IIT makes these benefits more widely available.

Wide and affordable availability of assistive devices such as DAISY can facilitate learning and employment opportunities for many. To further support as extensive as possible access and usage of the DAISY, software for the cataloging and maintenance of talking book libraries has also been developed. This software is aimed at the preparation and regular updating of common catalogues containing information about talking books available at talking book libraries around the country. The catalogue can be posted on the web, making the information easily available to the end user.

Finally, the NAB-INTEL Technology Unit has established an interest-free loan scheme for the trainees. This scheme was started with the help of HPS Social Welfare Foundation. A loan of up to Rs. 50,000 can be taken under this scheme, which is to be returned in a maximum of 18 equal instalments. Preference is given to those wishing to start up their own small business or who may receive employment as a result of having their own assistive technology tools.

C. Achievements

The NAB Computer Training Technology Centre was the first Computer Training Unit for the blind in India. Prior to the establishment of the Centre very few organizations believed in the potential of this technology. By establishing this Centre, and developing various training programmes and exploring the applicability ICT, a resource has been developed which can now be replicated anywhere in the country.

In the developing countries even the most basic of textbooks are often not available in Braille or audio format. The amount of material available for university students is negligible. NAB's computer education training has helped many blind or low-vision students overcome this barrier and take advantage of the new developments in ICT. Most importantly, it has assisted them in making the most of their right to accessible information. The large store of information and publications available through resources such as the Internet can now be read directly using a scanner. The biggest advantage is that a newspaper which is posted on a website can be accessible to a blind person without any conversion or reproduction. This has bridged the gap between the information available to the seeing and non-seeing world.

Perhaps the key feature and achievement of the programme has been the development of a strong effective collaboration between civil society and the corporate world. NAB's involvement in the programme ensured the participation of the user group in the development and conducting of the training course. INTEL provided economic stability to the programme and professional management systems, as well as ensuring the benefit reached a much larger group, especially the less privileged sections of society.

The partnership between NAB and INTEL has demonstrated the potential ICT has to transform the lives of people with disability and also their communities and workplaces. It has increased both potential employment opportunities and productivity of existing workers and workplaces.

One example of how this potential was capitalized on by NAB was its success in lobbying a major multinational company to take on blind staff members. Among its many operations, the company runs a call centre in India employing thousands of people. The operations could easily be managed by properly trained blind people. NAB successfully partnered with fellow NGO, Arushi, to lobby the Human Resources Department of the company to try employing persons with blindness and low-vision. The company agreed and a pilot project was started with two trainees. Within two months of their placement the trainees had achieved maximum levels of productivity, matching those of other employees, and convincing the company of the potential of non-seeing staff.

D. Key lessons learned

ICT is revolutionary technology for persons with blindness. To harness the potential of this technology, training is essential. It is necessary to have specialized training centres for the initiation process whilst advanced computer training is best in a non-specialized training environment.

E. Sustainability

ICT has had revolutionary consequences in enhancing the abilities and skills of persons with blindness. It is essential to create awareness of the opportunities provided by ICT. Many vision impaired persons are not able to make the most of this opportunity, however, because they are not aware of the latest assistive technology. The NAB-INTEL Technology Training Centre has undertaken many steps to raise awareness about this technology.

In addition, NAB has set up a second Centre with a wide range of assistive technologies. This Centre enables persons with vision impairment to have hands-on experience in the use of this technology. This assists in the correct identification of proper tools for them, and lessens the financial risk to users of buying costly equipment that is ill-matched to their needs.

Mastering computers and technology is a never-ending process. Sharing problems, finding more convenient ways of performing tasks etc., are things which can only be learned through discussions among peers in a cooperative learning environment. To this end the NAB Computer Training Centre initiated regular meetings of vision impaired computer users. This group has become a strong resource on how ICT can be used most effectively by persons with blindness or low-vision. The group provides support to each other and support and guidance to other blind users. Many important decisions on the future directions of the Computer Training and Technology Unit were taken in these group meetings.

PART SIX

HIGHLIGHTS OF THE ASIAN AND PACIFIC DECADE OF DISABLED PERSONS, 1993-2002

XVII. Socially Vulnerable Groups: Selected Issues: Empowerment of Persons with Disabilities

I n May 2002, ESCAP adopted resolution 58/4 on "Promoting an inclusive, barrier-free and rights-based society for people with disabilities in the Asian and Pacific region in the twenty-first century". The resolution also proclaimed the extension of the Asian and Pacific Decade of Disabled Persons, 1993-2002, for another decade, 2003-2012. In October 2002, Governments adopted the "Biwako Millennium Framework for Action towards an Inclusive, Barrier-free and Rights-based Society for Persons with Disabilities in Asian and the Pacific", (BMF) as the regional policy guideline for the new decade. By 2003, 43 members and associate members of ESCAP have signed the Proclamation on the Full Participation and Equality of People with Disabilities in the Asian and Pacific region. The new decade (2003-2012) must ensure the paradigm shift from a charity-based approach to a rights-based approach to protect the civil, cultural, economic, political, and social rights of persons with disabilities.

The attached paper on socially vulnerable groups: selected issues: empowerment of persons with disabilities, was presented to the Committee on Emerging Social Issues, held 4-6 September 2003 Bangkok. It summarizes the current status of persons with disabilities in the ESCAP region at the inception of the new Decade, the seven priority areas for action under the BMF, and its targets, strategies, timeframes and supporting/monitoring mechanisms as well as immediate ESCAP follow-up activities.

Despite recent achievements, persons with disabilities remain the single largest sector of those least-served and most discriminated against in almost all societies in the region. Persons with disabilities have been prevented from accessing entitlements available to other members of society, to health services, education, employment, community participation and other basic social and political rights and services. Failure to access these services, and to have their voices heard, has resulted in economic and social exclusion for persons with disabilities and their associates, prejudice, rejection and ultimately, lives in poverty.

There are a number of key areas that require ongoing critical action if the region is to satisfactorily achieve the inclusion of people with disabilities in society and in all mainstream development programmes in order to reach the goal of full participation of people with disabilities.

Economic and Social Commission for Asia and the Pacific

Committee on Emerging Social Issues

First session
4-6 September 2003
Bangkok

Socially Vulnerable Groups: Selected Issues: Empowerment of Persons with Disabilities

(Item 4(b) of the provisional agenda)

Note by the secretariat

SUMMARY

On 22 May 2002, the Commission adopted resolution 58/4 on promoting an inclusive, barrier-free and rights-based society for people with disabilities in the Asian and Pacific region in the twenty-first century, in which it proclaimed the extension of the Asian and Pacific Decade of Disabled Persons, 1993-2002, for another decade, 2003-2012. In October 2002, Governments adopted the Biwako Millennium Framework for Action towards an Inclusive, Barrier-free and Rights-based Society for Persons with Disabilities in Asia and the Pacific (BMF) as the regional policy guideline for the new Decade. As at 2003, 43 members and associate members of ESCAP have signed the Proclamation on the Full Participation and Equality of People with Disabilities in the Asian and Pacific Region. The new Decade (2003-2012) must ensure a paradigm shift from a charity-based approach to a rights-based approach to protect the civil, cultural, economic, political and social rights of persons with disabilities.

This paper summarizes the current status of persons with disabilities in the ESCAP region at the inception of the new Decade, the seven priority areas for action under BMF and its targets, strategies, time-frames and supporting/monitoring mechanisms as well as immediate ESCAP follow-up activities.

Despite recent achievements, persons with disabilities remain the single-largest sector of those least served and most discriminated against in almost all societies in the region. Persons with disabilities have been prevented from accessing entitlements available to other members of society, in the areas of health services, education, employment, community participation and other basic social and political rights and services. Failure to access these services, and to have their voices heard, has resulted in economic and social exclusion for persons with disabilities and their associates, prejudice, rejection and, ultimately, lives in poverty.

There are a number of key areas that require ongoing critical action if the region is to satisfactorily achieve the inclusion of people with disabilities in society and in all mainstream development programmes in order to reach the goal of full participation of people with disabilities.

Introduction

1.   On 22 May 2002, the Commission adopted resolution 58/4 on promoting an inclusive, barrier-free and rights-based society for people with disabilities in the Asian and Pacific region in the twenty-first century, in which it proclaimed the extension of the Asian and Pacific Decade of Disabled Persons, 1993-2002, for another decade, 2003-2012.

2.   In October 2002, the High-level Intergovernmental Meeting to Conclude the Asian and Pacific Decade of Disabled Persons, 1993-2002, adopted the Biwako Millennium Framework for Action towards an Inclusive, Barrier-free and Rights-based Society for Persons with Disabilities in Asia and the Pacific (BMF) as the regional policy guideline for the new Decade.

3.   The Biwako Millennium Framework outlines issues, action plans and strategies towards an inclusive, barrier-free and rights-based society for persons with disabilities.

4.   To achieve the goals, the Framework identified seven priority areas for action, in each of which critical issues and targets with specific time frames and actions follow. In all, 21 targets and 17 strategies supporting the achievement of the targets were identified.

5.   As at 2003, 43 members and associate members of ESCAP have signed the Proclamation on the Full Participation and Equality of People with Disabilities in the Asian and Pacific Region.

6.   The new Decade (2003-2012) must ensure a paradigm shift from a charity-based approach to a rights-based approach to protect the civil, cultural, economic, political and social rights of persons with disabilities. To pursue the targets and strategies, consultations with and involvement of civil society, including self-help organizations (SHOs) and concerned NGOs, are essential.

7.   The following sections of this paper summarize the current status of persons with disabilities in the ESCAP region at the inception of the new Decade, the seven priority areas for action under BMF and its targets, strategies, time frames and supporting/monitoring mechanisms as well as immediate ESCAP follow-up activities. The first Asian and Pacific Decade of Disabled Persons was concluded in 2002. The theme and goal of the Decade was the promotion of the full participation and equality of people with disabilities in the Asian and Pacific region.

8.   The paper also summarizes the achievements of the last Decade, its shortcomings and challenges, and priority areas for further action during the new Decade. The focus of analysis is on progress at the national level, which may be used as a baseline for monitoring future progress.

9.   Information has been derived mainly from a regional survey conducted by ESCAP for the above-mentioned High-level Intergovernmental Meeting in 2002 and other supplementary data provided by additional meeting reports and background documents on related activities that took place in 2002 and 2003. The former survey report is based on 37 returns of the ESCAP survey questionnaire, including from four non-signatories of the Proclamation.

I. Overview of the Current Situation

10.   It is recognized that many gains have been achieved in creating awareness about the situation of persons with disabilities in the Asian and Pacific region and the need to address the issues affecting their full participation and equality in the development process. There has been progress at the national and subregional levels, where a variety of measures for equalization are being implemented. These include legislation, promotion of barrier-free environments, community-based rehabilitation services, education and training and employment. People with disabilities are increasingly active in contributing to the planning and implementation of programmes relating to such measures.

11.   Despite these achievements, it may be argued that persons with disabilities remain the single-largest sector of those least served and most discriminated against in almost all societies in the region.

12.   Persons with disabilities have been prevented from accessing entitlements available to other members of society, in the areas of health services, education, employment, community participation and other basic social and political rights and services. Failure to access these services and to have their voices heard has resulted in economic and social exclusion for persons with disabilities and their associates, prejudice, rejection and, ultimately, lives in poverty. The number of persons with disabilities continues to increase with population growth and such other factors as war and other forms of violence, traffic accidents, inadequate medical care and natural and other disasters.

13.   There are a number of key areas that require ongoing critical action if the region is to satisfactorily achieve the inclusion of people with disabilities in society and in all mainstream development programmes in order to reach the goal of full participation of people with disabilities. Not surprisingly, many of the people with disabilities are poor; poverty and social exclusion are closely linked.

14.   The overwhelming majority of people with disabilities in the ESCAP region live in remote rural areas where the services needed to help them are unavailable. Additionally, a major cause of poverty is the lack of productive employment.

15.   People with disabilities remain disproportionately unemployed and underemployed. Efforts have been made in many parts of the ESCAP region to improve the labour force participation rate but a major obstacle to gaining – and retaining – employment is lack of access to education and training. People with disabilities are confronted with social exclusion from their earliest years because of existing social and physical barriers.

16.   Generally, the educational systems fail to offer any education to the majority of children with disabilities. Among those who do have access to education, few receive inclusive education in the mainstream school environment. Additionally, an increasingly important issue in this area that still has to be addressed is access by people with disabilities to new and emerging information technologies through computer literacy.

17.   Since lack of education is one of the main factors leading to social exclusion and poverty, this phenomenon will be followed by new emerging problems related to ICT developments, globalization and poverty, including temporary poverty caused by structural adjustments.

18.   It is hoped that the extension of the Asian and Pacific Decade of Disabled Persons for another 10 years will complete the achievement of the goal of full participation and equality of people with disabilities.

A. Self-help organizations of persons with disabilities and related family and parents' associations

19.   Governments in the ESCAP region are becoming increasingly supportive of SHOs and value the role which they play in advising Governments on disability concerns. Twenty-four countries out of 37 that responded to the ESCAP survey have formed national cross-disability organizations of people with disabilities, or SHOs. Four were in the process of forming such groups. The World Blind Union and the World Federation of the Deaf have extensive networks of national organizations.

20.   Seventeen Governments have reported that input by SHOs was fully integrated into national policy development. Thirteen Governments provide funding assistance to strengthen and support the development of SHOs. The Philippines has a national forum of SHOs. In the Pacific island economies, the Oceania Subregional Office of Disabled Peoples' International (DPI) was formed in 2000 and provides support to many countries in the subregion. DPI Asia and Pacific region has a membership of 22 national assemblies of people with disabilities. These include six organizations from the Pacific island economies.

21.   Some SHOs have developed without government support, as in Kiribati and Solomon Islands, but they helped to improve public attitudes towards persons with disabilities. Additionally, the lack of coordination of many disparate and often single-disability groups has weakened the capacity of SHOs to advocate their cause effectively. Coordination is clearly beneficial to people with disabilities and Governments alike. A situation of equal partnership and consultation between Governments and SHOs has not yet been achieved within the region and progress towards it has been slow.

22.   Often, SHOs have not yet fully included marginalized persons with disabilities such as women and girls with disabilities, persons with intellectual disabilities and persons with psychiatric disabilities.

23.   BMF affirms that persons with disabilities and their SHOs are best equipped and best informed to speak on their behalf and can contribute to solutions on issues that concern them. Under BMF, two targets are set to make a difference:

(1) By 2004, Governments, international funding agencies and NGOs should establish policies to support and develop SHOs Governments should take steps to ensure the formation of parents' associations at the local level by the year 2005 and federate them at the national level by year 2010;

(2) By 2005, Governments and civil society organizations should fully include SHOs in decision-making processes.

24.   Actions for the targets include the participation of persons with disabilities in policy-making, political representations and capacity-building.

B. Women with disabilities

25.   Some countries have developed gender-inclusive disability policies while others facilitate gender-sensitive data and the formation of networks of women with disabilities. These initiatives need to continue and expand if women with disabilities are to acquire the skills and confidence to advocate for the inclusion of their particular issues within SHOs of persons with disabilities, mainstream advocacy groups and the wider community.

26.   Gender-inclusive disability policies were reported by Japan, the Philippines and Sri Lanka. Gender-sensitive data were reported by Pakistan. Bangladesh; Bhutan; Fiji; Hong Kong, China; Indonesia; and the Philippines reported the formation of networks of women with disabilities. A regional network of women with disabilities was formed at Hanoi during Campaign 2001. In Fiji, the group of women with disabilities is a member of the Fiji National Council of Women. The Fiji Disabled Peoples' Association has a task force on women. In the Philippines, a leadership training manual for women with disabilities has been developed, and ongoing training is carried out.

27.   Given that women with disabilities suffer doubly from being women and from being disabled, it is clear that the concerns and development of women with disabilities should form a central part of any future framework for action in the region.

28.   In BMF, women with disabilities are recognized as multiply disadvantaged through their status as women and as persons with disabilities and their propensity to be living in poverty. Three targets are set to solve these problems:

    (1) By 2005, Governments should ensure anti-discrimination measures, where appropriate, to protect women with disabilities;

    (2) By 2005, SHOs should adopt policies to promote full representation of women with disabilities;

    (3) By 2005, women with disabilities should be included in the membership of national mainstream women's associations.

C. Early detection, early intervention and education

29.   Twenty-five countries out of 37 survey respondents have prevention strategies within overall health programmes, while comprehensive disability prevention programmes were implemented in Bangladesh, China and India, among others. In China, nationwide prevention strategies target urban, rural and migrant communities. National surveys of children at risk have been undertaken and early identification and intervention services provide training and support to families in 23 countries and areas, within urban and community-based frameworks. Prevention programmes included safety in the workplace and the prevention of traffic accidents and, in some cases, injury due to landmines. In 2001 the Government of New Zealand released a strategy on the health of older people with a view to supporting positive ageing and prevention of disability.

30.   Continued effort is needed to further reduce the number of infants born with disabilities as a result of maternal malnutrition, inadequate prenatal and post-natal care, childbirth complications and preventable childhood diseases.

31.   Twenty-nine countries out of 37 provide for rehabilitation services and 22 have established community-based rehabilitation (CBR) approaches. In one notable model in Bangladesh, three government departments work together with more than 100 NGOs and some organizations of people with disabilities to provide rehabilitation to people with disabilities within their community. Deliberate policy decisions have resulted in extensive CBR service delivery in China, India, Indonesia, Malaysia and the Philippines and rapidly expanding services in Solomon Islands, Sri Lanka, Thailand and Viet Nam.

32.   However, many rehabilitation services in the region are still urban and institution-based. They lack consultative and participatory mechanisms that would allow people with disabilities and their families a role as equal partners in problem-solving.

33.   It is estimated that well under 10 per cent of children with disabilities in developing countries have access to education. Lack of data on the number and prevalence of children with disabilities makes it impossible to measure progress or gain a better understanding of these issues.

34.   There is some evidence that the situation is improving. Legislation mandating education for all children has been passed or is being planned by 20 Governments. However, only a few Governments provided for the inclusion of children with disabilities in national Education for All plans. The predominant form of access to education has been through separate school provision, but inclusive educational provision was increasing. Twenty-seven Governments reported some access to regular schools for children and youth with disabilities.

35.   It is roughly estimated that less than 10 per cent of children and youth with disabilities have access to any form of education, compared with an enrolment rate of over 70 per cent for non-disabled children and youth in primary education in the region. This exclusion from education for children and youth with disabilities results in exclusion from opportunity for further personal, social and vocational development. Four targets are set for these problems:

    (1) Children with disabilities will be an integral part of the population targeted by Millennium Development Goal target 3, which is to ensure that, by 2015, children everywhere, boys and girls alike, will be able to complete a full course of primary schooling;

    (2) By 2010, at least 75 per cent of children and youth with disabilities of school age will be able to complete a full course of primary schooling;

    (3) By 2012, all infants and young children (0-4 years) will have access to and receive community-based early intervention services;

    (4) Governments should ensure detection of childhood disabilities at a very early age.

36.   Actions in this area include adequate legislation for inclusive education and national data collection on children with disabilities (0-16 years).

D. Access to built environments and public transport

37.   Some progress has been made in this area, with 24 Governments having adopted, or being in the progress of developing, legislation and standards on accessible environments and transport.

38.   Inaccessibility of the built environment, including public transport systems, is still the major barrier for persons with disabilities. This problem will get worse, as the number of older people with disabilities increases in the region. A new inclusive, integral approach, "universal design", benefits all people in our society including older persons, pregnant women and young children and its economic benefits have been proved; yet substantive initiatives at the policy level have not been taken. Three targets are set to improve the situation:

(1) Governments should adopt and enforce accessibility standards for the planning of public facilities, infrastructure and transport, including those in rural/agricultural contexts;

(2) Existing public transport systems and all new and renovated public transport systems should be made accessible as soon as practicable;

(3) All international and regional funding agencies for infrastructure development should include universal and inclusive design concepts in their loan/grant award criteria.

E. Training and employment, including self-employment

39.   Of 28 Governments which provide vocational training services, 5 were in the early stages of establishing such services. Nine countries are moving towards integrated provision of vocational training. Many strategies had been adopted to promote increased rates of employment of people with disabilities. Twelve countries have implemented a quota system with incentives and fines being used to ensure enforcement. Additional strategies include job search agencies, employment placement and support centres, wage subsidies, job coaching, trial employment and industrial profiling.

40.   Strategies to promote self-employment and income generation through small grant funding, microcredit and loans have been reported in a number of countries. These countries and others reported a specific focus on employment of people with disabilities in rural areas. The Government of Japan has begun employment promotion for people with severe disabilities within the private sector.

41.   Nevertheless, persons with disabilities remain disproportionately undereducated, untrained, unemployed, underemployed and poor. They have insufficient access to the mainstream labour market owing to social exclusion, lack of trained and competent staff and adequate training for independent workers.

42.   By 2003, only 11 countries in the region had ratified ILO Convention concerning Vocational Rehabilitation and Employment (Disabled Persons), 1983. Three targets follow:

(1) By 2012, at least 30 per cent of the signatories will ratify ILO Convention concerning Vocational Rehabilitation and Employment (Disabled Persons);

(2) By 2012, at least 30 per cent of all vocational training programmes in signatory countries will include persons with disabilities;

(3) By 2010, reliable data on the employment and self-employment rates of persons with disabilities will exist in all countries.

F. Access to information and communications, including information, communication and assistive technologies

43.   In terms of access to communication, there is wide use of Braille and sign language, with popular usage and access by hearing people in countries such as China and Thailand. National sign language dictionaries were developed, and in 1999 in Thailand sign language was declared the national language of deaf people.

44.   Overall access to communications technology and computer literacy in the region is clearly limited and not available to the majority of people with disabilities, especially those living in rural areas or in urban poverty. In terms of accessible information and ICT-related services, much more needs to be done. Where related ICT legislation has been passed, it is often not enforced.

45.   In the past 10 years, there has been much progress in ICT development in some countries of the region, and this opens up many opportunities for people with disabilities in networking, solidarity, employment and independent living.

46.   Advances in ICT have also widened the gap between privileged disabled persons and non-privileged ones, as well as persons with disabilities and the non-disabled. The digital divide includes inaccessibility of infrastructure for ICT and the Internet, as well as English language skills. These problems are acute in rural areas. The multimedia environment and graphics-based electronic information are creating new forms of barriers for people with visual disabilities.

47.   Based on information from a disability survey in the Republic of Korea (the most advanced ICT environment in the region) which revealed that persons with disabilities have 75 per cent less opportunity to access the Internet than non-disabled persons, legislation has been passed to implement measures to redress the imbalance in computer literacy between persons with and without disabilities. Japan has issued information accessibility guidelines for Japanese personal computer manufacturers, thus involving the private sector as a partner. Accessibility was reported as an emerging concern in Hong Kong, China; Thailand; and Turkey, where free access to computers was made available.

48.   Indeed, access to communications technology and computer literacy has the capacity to transform the lives of persons with disabilities, greatly enhancing their capacity to pursue gainful livelihoods. Five targets are set to improve the situation:

(1)   By 2005, persons with disabilities should have at least the same rate of access to the Internet and related services as other citizens in a country;

(2)   By 2004, international organizations should incorporate accessibility standards for persons with disabilities into their international ICT standards;

(3)   Governments should adopt, by 2005, ICT accessibility guidelines for persons with disabilities in their national ICT policies;

(4)   Governments should develop and coordinate a standardized sign language and finger Braille in each country and disseminate and teach the results through all means, i.e., publications, CD-ROMs, etc.;

(5)   Governments should establish a system in each country to train and dispatch sign language interpreters, Braille transcribers, finger Braille interpreters and human readers and to encourage their productive employment.

G. Poverty alleviation through capacity-building, social security and sustainable livelihood programmes

49.   Increasingly the link between poverty and disability and the unmet needs of the majority of disabled persons living in rural areas is being recognized. The capacities of persons with disabilities must be developed so that they may contribute to community-based solutions to the particular problems that they face. Governments need to ensure that vulnerable persons with disabilities are able to access health, education, training and employment services and are integrated into community development programmes. The low rates of access to appropriate education for children with disabilities and high rates of unemployment for youth and adults with disabilities in rural areas both need urgent attention.

50.   Persons with disabilities are the poorest of the poor. It is estimated that 160 million persons with disabilities in the region, over 40 per cent of the total, are living in poverty, unable to benefit from their socio-economic rights. It is also estimated that 70 to 80 per cent of people with disabilities in some countries of the region live below the national poverty line.

51.   Research has found that a higher proportion of households having members with disabilities were living below the poverty line and had lower total assets, smaller land holdings and greater debt than households without disabled members. The unemployment rate has been at least twice or even three times that of non-disabled people. When disabled people are employed, there is a greater tendency for them to be underemployed relative to their levels of training.

52.   Malnutrition in its various forms is a cause of disability as well as a contributory factor in other ailments that increase susceptibility to disabling diseases. According to the Food and Agriculture Organization of the United Nations, there are currently 515 million Asians chronically undernourished, accounting for about two thirds of the world's hungry people.

53.   Poverty and disability worsen each other when persons with disabilities are socially excluded and adequate social services are not provided.

54.   The extra costs directly related to disability can be considerable. In India, a survey found that the direct cost of treatment and equipment varied from three days' to two years' income, with a mean of two months.

55.   Pursuant to the United Nations Millennium Development Goal target 1, Governments should halve, between 1990 and 2015, the proportion of persons with disabilities whose income/consumption is less than one dollar a day. Governments should integrate disability dimensions into MDG baseline data collection and analysis and allocate a certain percentage of the total rural development/poverty alleviation funds to persons with disabilities.

H. Disability statistics and research

56.   The establishment of national databases is essential to provide accurate information on people with disabilities and their situations, without which it is difficult to plan appropriate services and monitor progress towards the achievement of full participation and equality.

57.   Many Governments have taken action to collect data on disabilities. Ten Governments have developed a national disability database and five Governments are planning to develop one. Some countries have data collection to include information on children with disabilities vis-à-vis education, others a database focused on industrial profiles and job opportunities for people with disabilities. Five Governments have established databases to collect information on users of various services available to people with disabilities.

58.   In the Pacific island economies, comprehensive and specific disability surveys were undertaken in some areas and further surveys are planned for others. The Republic of Korea has been conducting national surveys on disability every five years, the findings of which have supported policy changes to address disability issues.

59.   There still remain many problems in this area: data collection is not transparent in some contexts; it does not reflect the full extent of disability and this renders comparison of data meaningless. These limitations are due in part to the conceptual framework adopted, the scope and coverage of the surveys undertaken and the definitions, classifications and methodology used.

60.   A common system of definition and classification of disability is not uniformly applied in the region. Two strategies are set to solve the problem. Strategy 8 of BMF calls for Governments to develop, by 2005, their system for disability-related data collection and analysis. Strategy 9 calls for Governments to adopt, by 2005, definitions on disability based on the United Nations publication, *Guidelines and Principles for the Development of Disability Statistics.*

I. Rights-based legislation

61.   Thirteen Governments out of 37 survey respondents have adopted comprehensive disability legislation, 9 Governments reported that legislation was in preparation and 27 have enacted, or are in the process of revising, extensive additional specific legislation or regulations. Measures for the enforcement and enactment of anti-discrimination legislation have also been undertaken by a number of Governments.

62.   Several good practices of national laws are found in the Law of China, the 1991 Act of Thailand, the Magna Carta in the Philippines and related national laws in Bangladesh, Sri Lanka and Viet Nam. The new Constitution of Timor-Leste, which was adopted in August 2001, includes two articles that refer to the rights of people with disabilities.

63.   A major challenge in this area is the establishment of stricter mechanisms for the enforcement of legislation and the application of penalties for non-compliance.

64.   Strategy 2 of BMF calls for Governments to examine the adoption and implementation of non-discrimination policies. Strategy 3 draws attention to national human rights institutions as agencies to protect disabled people's rights. Strategy 4 calls for Governments to actively involve persons with disabilities in policy development. Strategy 5 calls for Governments to consider ratifying the core international human rights treaties. Strategy 6 calls for Governments to consider support for the Ad Hoc Committee on a Comprehensive and Integral International Convention on Protection and Promotion of the Rights and Dignity of Persons with Disabilities. Strategy 7 calls on Governments to include persons with disabilities and their organizations, in their procedures at the national, regional and international levels, concerning the drafting and adoption of the proposed human rights convention on disability.

III. ESCAP Activities During 2003

65.   Taking into consideration the above-mentioned conditions and targets, ESCAP has programmed well-focused activities to be undertaken during 2003, in the following areas:

(a)   An international convention to protect and promote the rights and dignity of persons with disabilities;

(b)   Access to information and ICT;

(c)   Women and disability;

(d)   Access to built environments;

(e)   Poverty and disability;

(f)   Regional networking;

(g)   Disability statistics.

A. An international convention to protect and promote the rights and dignity of persons with disabilities

66.   In 2003, three consecutive activities have been planned on the elaboration of an international convention. First, an Expert Group Meeting and Seminar on an International Convention to Protect and Promote the Rights and Dignity of Persons with Disabilities was held at Bangkok from 2 to 4 June 2003.

67.   In pursuance of previous United Nations resolutions, this Expert Group Meeting and Seminar was held to generate a regional input to the elaboration of an international convention on the rights of persons with disabilities. It increased awareness and interest among civil society organizations, particularly human rights NGOs, and Governments in the region with regard to the international convention. The training seminar component of this activity greatly helped to empower people with disabilities themselves by enhancing their knowledge of the human rights issues and negotiation skills, and to ensure their active participation in the national process of elaborating the convention.

68.   As requested in General Assembly resolution 57/229 of 18 December 2002, the recommendations of this Expert Group Meeting and Seminar (Bangkok recommendations) were made available by ESCAP to the Ad Hoc Committee at its second session, held in New York from 16 to 27 June 2003.

69.   It will also serve as a main background document for two forthcoming meetings on the subject to be organized by ESCAP during the second half of this year, at Bangkok (October) and Beijing (November).

70.   The participants in the first Bangkok Expert Group Meeting were convinced that a new international human rights treaty was necessary to ensure that persons with disabilities fully enjoy their human rights in the region.

71.   Notwithstanding possible limitations and shortcomings, the move towards a new international convention for people with disabilities will have positive effects on Governments in the region and their development of anti-discriminatory national laws and policies to protect and promote the rights of persons with disabilities.

B. Access to information and ICT

72.   From 2003 forward, all ESCAP regional meetings and workshops on disability will utilize the standard format of accessible electronic reporting, including e-proceedings and virtual on-line discussion with a fully accessible standard format of web site home pages and CDs to accommodate the special needs of blind end-users. In 2003, ESCAP and the Asia-Pacific Development Center on Disability (APCD) co-organized a regional workshop on accessible web page-based networking for people with disabilities.

C. Women and disability

73.   Strengthening the capacity of women with disabilities and their organizations is a priority if persons with disabilities are to take responsibility for their own development, in partnership with Governments and NGOs.

74.   ESCAP is implementing a project designed to provide a good package of advocacy skills by organizing two consecutive training workshops targeting mainly women with disabilities. The workshops' agenda will cover the BMF targets and enhance the understanding of the concept of gender mainstreaming among NGOs and SHOs of persons with disabilities so that they will be familiar with and accept BMF and be motivated to take the necessary actions to achieve the BMF goals, particularly those related to women and disability. Beneficiaries will include policy makers of national and international NGOs and SHOs in addition to some governmental organizations. The project will promote a rights-based approach through training sessions to generate unified ESCAP regional support for the ongoing process of elaborating an international convention on the rights of persons with disabilities.

75.   This project is devised to provide advocacy skills for women with disabilities to participate actively in the national, regional and global efforts towards an international convention on protection and promotion of the rights and dignity of persons with disabilities, taking into consideration international and regional instruments and norms such as the 1993 Standard Rules on the Equalization of Opportunities for Persons with Disabilities.

76.   The recommendations from the planned workshops will be incorporated into the ESCAP regional meeting on the international convention to be held in October and provide a vital regional input to future global sessions of the Ad Hoc Committee on a Comprehensive and Integral International Convention on Protection and Promotion of the Rights and Dignity of Persons with Disabilities.

D. Access to built environments

77.   ESCAP and APCD co-organized the Regional Training of Trainers Course on the Promotion of Non-handicapping Environments for Persons with Disabilities at Bangkok from 24 February to 11 March 2003.

78.   ESCAP joined the Royal Thai Government and the Japan International Cooperation Agency (JICA) through APCD to organize this training workshop of trainers to strengthen capabilities in improving access in ESCAP developing countries. Beginning this year, APCD will be the main organizer of this training course. APCD is a joint initiative of the Government of Thailand and the Government of Japan through JICA. APCD was established as a legacy of the Asian and Pacific Decade of Disabled Persons concluded in 2002. Around 30 participants from nine countries, including policy makers, architects, urban planners and persons with disabilities attended this two-week training session.

E. Poverty and disability

79.   ESCAP collaborated with the Colombo Plan Secretariat in organizing a training workshop on raising awareness on mainstreaming disability rights and concerns into national development across all sectors from 24 to 29 March 2003. The training was specifically designed for public sector officials in decision-making positions.

80.   Some 20 participants from Colombo Plan member countries participated in the workshop. They experienced an extensive and intensive one-week training course that included a field visit to a slum area of Bangkok, exposure to an interactive panel discussion by leading local disability advocates and a disability experiential exercise, which sensitized them to issues of physical access in the built environment. The participants prepared action plans for implementation on return to their home countries.

81.   The participants noted some recent improvements in mainstreaming disability issues into pro-poor development strategies and in formulating comprehensive development policies targeting persons with disabilities and their families at the national level. However, they felt that progress had been uneven and limited, and the majority of people with disabilities were prevented from receiving adequate food, balanced nutrition, productive employment and other very basic social services such as access to safe drinking water and sanitation.

82.   The course curriculum covered such critical issues as (a) disability, poverty and development, (b) access to basic social services, (c) promotion of participation of persons with disabilities through social mobilization, (d) promotion of employment and income generation activities and (e) coordination mechanisms and multisectoral convergence. The policy makers particularly valued the experiential disability simulation exercise and the opportunity to visit the Klong Toey slum community in Bangkok, where they gained first-hand knowledge of the challenges faced by poor families with a disabled family member.

F. Regional networking

83.   ESCAP has been organizing biannual sessions of the Thematic Working Group on Disability-related Concerns. The first session in 2003 was held at Bangkok on 5 and 6 June 2003. The Group's primary objective is to sustain the momentum towards the fulfilment of the BMF goals in the new Decade. The position of co-chairperson has been held by ESCAP, other United Nations agencies and NGOs. The membership has expanded to include 50 NGOs, some 15 government representatives and the Asian Development Bank. The Group had been active in setting targets for the final period of the first Decade and in reviewing the achievements in the implementation of the Agenda for Action.

84. The Group was instrumental in advocating the extension of the Decade, 2003-2012. Members were actively engaged in assisting ESCAP in drafting BMF. Several task forces have been formed to promote advocacy and action in fulfilment of the particular BMF targets in such areas as Education for All, including children with disabilities; employment and training; access to information and ICT; emerging issues in Timor-Leste and Afghanistan; an international convention; women and disability; and SHOs. These task forces have been very effective in raising awareness of the need to include children with disabilities in national education, promoting inclusion of concerns of persons with disabilities in regional ICT meetings and facilitating funding for a project to support national survey and disability awareness in Timor-Leste.

G. Disability statistics

85. Lack of data makes it difficult to assess improvements achieved during the Asian and Pacific Decade of Disabled Persons. Clearly, further action is needed to achieve full participation and equality.

86. ESCAP is organizing a training workshop on disability measurement. ESCAP is attempting to offer selected member countries a forum where they can meet to discuss their problems related to measuring disability, including various issues such as definitions, classifications, standardization, data collection, sampling, reporting and identification of selected good policy indicators for monitoring purposes. The workshop could also contribute to ensuring that the Asian and Pacific perspective is taken into consideration in international disability initiatives such as the Washington Group on Disability Measurement. Currently, Australia is the only country in the region that has participated in the first two meetings of the Washington Group on Disability Measurement.

IV. Future Challenges

87.   Achievement of the theme and goal of the new Decade is still at its very initial stages. Progress made during the first Decade was so uneven that most of the key goals of BMF will pose serious challenges in the years ahead.

88.   The establishment of national statistical databases is essential to provide accurate information on people with disabilities and their situations, without which it is almost impossible to plan appropriate services and monitor progress towards the achievement of the goals. Excluded from education, people with disabilities are excluded from other opportunities and development, and condemned to live in poverty.

89.   Strengthening of the capacities of women with disabilities and their organizations is a priority if persons with disabilities (both men and women) are to take responsibility for their own development, in a participatory manner and in a sustainable and mutually reinforcing partnership with Governments and NGOs.

90.   Strong commitment by the Governments of the region with full regional cooperation is needed to ensure that the equal rights of all people with disabilities, including the right to participate in development and decision-making, are fully achieved in Asian and Pacific societies by 2012. By the year 2012 it is hoped that the goals of the Biwako Millennium Framework will largely have been achieved.

ANNEX

Asian and Pacific
Decade of Disabled Persons, 2003-2012

Biwako Millennium Framework
for Action: towards an Inclusive,
Barrier-free and Rights-based Society
for Persons with Disabilities
in Asia and the Pacific

Lake "Biwa" is the largest freshwater lake in Japan, in the City of Otsu. It is in this city that the High-level Intergovernmental Meeting to Conclude the Asian and Pacific Decade of Disabled Persons was held. Hence, the name of the framework is "Biwako" ("ko" means a lake). The word "Millennium" indicates that the Framework was adopted at the beginning of the new millennium and also that it is structured to supplement the United Nations Millennium Development Goals and targets. "An Inclusive, Barrier-free and Rights-based Society" represents the guiding principles of this framework. An "inclusive" society is a society for all, and a "barrier-free" society refers to a society free from institutional, physical and attitudinal barriers, as well as social, economic and cultural barriers. A "rights-based" society means a society based on the human rights of all individuals where peoples with disabilities are valued and placed at the centre of all decisions affecting them.

In May 2002, ESCAP adopted the resolution "Promoting an inclusive, barrier-free and rights-based society for people with disabilities in the Asian and Pacific region in the twenty-first century". The resolution also proclaimed the extension of the Asian and Pacific Decade of Disabled Persons, 1993-2002, for another decade, 2003-2012.

In October 2002, Governments at the High-level Intergovernmental Meeting to Conclude the Asian and Pacific Decade of Disabled Persons 1993-2002, adopted the "Biwako Millennium Framework for Action towards an Inclusive, Barrier-free and Rights-based Society for Persons with Disabilities in Asian and the Pacific", as the regional policy guideline for the new decade.

The "Biwako Millennium Framework" outlines issues, action plans and strategies towards an inclusive, barrier-free and rights-based society for persons with disabilities.

To achieve the goal, the framework identifies seven priority areas for action, in each of which critical issues, targets with specific timeframes, and actions are specified. In all, 21 targets and 17 strategies supporting the achievement of all the targets are identified.

The new decade (2003-2012) will ensure the paradigm shift from a charity-based approach to a rights-based approach to protect the civil, cultural, economic, political, and social rights of persons with disabilities.

To pursue the targets and strategies, consultations with and involvement of civil society, inter alia, self-help organizations and concerned NGOs are essential.

The following sections summarize the seven priority areas for action, the targets, strategies, time-frames, and the supporting/monitoring mechanisms.

A. Self-help organizations of persons with disabilities and related family and parent associations

Persons with disabilities and their self-help organizations are the most equipped and best informed to speak on their behalf and can contribute to solutions on issues that concern them. Two targets are set to make the difference:

(1) By 2004, Governments, international funding agencies and NGOs should establish policy to support and develop self-help organizations. Governments should take steps to ensure the formation of parents associations at local levels by the year 2005 and federate them at the national level by year 2010.

(2) By 2005, Governments and civil society organizations should fully include self-help organizations in decision-making processes.

Actions for the targets include the participation of persons with disabilities in policy-making, political representations and capacity building.

Self-help organizations should include marginalized persons with disabilities such as women and girls with disabilities, persons with intellectual disabilities and persons with psychiatric disabilities.

B. Women with disabilities

Women with disabilities are multiply disadvantaged through their status as women, as persons with disabilities, and their likelihood to be living in poverty. Three targets are set to solve these problems:

(1) By 2005, Governments should ensure anti-discrimination measures, where appropriate, to protect women with disabilities.

(2) By 2005, self-help organizations should adopt policies to promote full representation of women with disabilities.

(3) By 2005, women with disabilities should be included in the membership of national mainstream women's associations.

C. Early detection, early intervention and education

Fewer than 10 per cent of children and youth with disabilities have access to any form of education compared with an enrolment rate of over 70 per cent for non-disabled children and youth in primary education in the Asian and Pacific region. This exclusion from education for children and youth with disabilities results in exclusion from opportunity for further personal, social and vocational development. Four targets are set for these problems:

(1) Children with disabilities will be an integral part of the population targeted by Millennium Development Goal Target 3, which is to ensure that, by 2015, children everywhere, boys and girls alike, will be able to complete a full course of primary schooling.

(2) By 2010, at least 75 per cent of children and youth with disabilities of school age will be able to complete a full course of primary schooling.

(3) By 2012, all infants and young children (0-4 years) will have access to and receive community-based early intervention services.

(4) Governments should ensure detection of childhood disabilities at a very early age.

Actions in this area include adequate legislation for inclusive education and national data collection on children with disabilities (0-16 years).

D. Training and employment, including self employment

Persons with disabilities remain disproportionately undereducated, untrained, unemployed, underemployed and poor. They have insufficient access to the mainstream labour market partially due to social exclusion, lack of trained and competent staff and adequate training for independent workers. Three targets follow:

(1) By 2012, at least 30 per cent of the signatories (member states) will ratify ILO Convention 159 concerning Vocational Rehabilitation and Employment (Disabled Persons).

(2) By 2012, at least 30 per cent of all vocational training programmes in signatory countries will include persons with disabilities.

(3) By 2010, reliable data on the employment and self-employment rates of persons with disabilities will exist in all countries.

E. Access to built environment and public transport

Inaccessibility to the built environment, including public transport systems, is still the major barrier for persons with disabilities. This problem will only be exacerbated, as the number of older people with disabilities increases in the region. Universal design approaches benefit all people in society, including older persons, pregnant women and parents with young children. Its economic benefits have been legitimized, yet substantive initiatives at policy level have not been taken. Three targets are set to improve the situation:

(1) Governments should adopt and enforce accessibility standards for planning of public facilities, infrastructure and transport, including those in rural/agricultural contexts.

(2) Existing public transport systems and all new and renovated public transport systems should be made accessible as soon as practicable.

(3) All international and regional funding agencies for infrastructure development should include universal and inclusive design concepts in their loan/grant award criteria.

F. Access to information and communications, including information, communication and assistive technologies

In the past 10 years, there has been much progress in information and communication technology (ICT) development, and it opens up many opportunities for people with disabilities in networking, solidarity, employment and independent living. But it has also widened the gap between persons with disabilities and the non-disabled. The digital divide includes inaccessibility to infrastructure for ICT, Internet, and ICT skills. These problems are acute in rural areas. The multimedia environment is creating barriers for people with visual disabilities. Five targets are set to improve the situation:

(1) By 2005, persons with disabilities should have at least the same rate of access to the Internet and related services as the rest of citizens in a country of the region.

(2) By 2004, international organizations should incorporate accessibility standards for persons with disabilities in their international ICT standards.

(3) Governments should adopt, by 2005, ICT accessibility guidelines for persons with disabilities in their national ICT policies.

(4) Governments should develop and coordinate a standardized sign language, finger Braille (tactile sign language), in each country and disseminate and teach the results through all means, i.e. publications, CD-ROMs, etc.

(5) Governments should establish a system in each country to train and dispatch sign language interpreters, Braille transcribers, finger Braille interpreters, and human readers and to encourage their productive employment.

G. Poverty alleviation through social security and livelihood programmes

Persons with disabilities are the poorest of the poor. It is estimated that 160 million persons with disabilities (over 40 per cent of the total) are living in poverty, unable to benefit from their socio-economic rights. Poverty and disability are mutually reinforcing as persons with disabilities are socially excluded and adequate social services are not provided. Pursuant to the United Nations Millennium Development Goal target 1:

(1) Governments should halve, between 1990 and 2015, the proportion of persons with disabilities whose income/consumption is less than one dollar a day. Actions call for Governments to integrate disability dimensions into MDG baseline data collection and analysis, to allocate a certain percentage of the total rural development/poverty alleviation funds towards persons with disabilities.

National plan of action (five-year) on disability

Strategy 1 calls for Governments to develop and adopt, by 2004, a five-year comprehensive national plan of action to implement the targets and strategies of the framework.

Promotion of rights-based approach to disability issues

Strategy 2 calls for Governments to examine the adoption and implementation non-discrimination policies. Strategy 3 draws attention to National Human Rights Institutions as agencies to protect disabled people's rights. Strategy 4 calls for Governments to actively involve persons with disabilities in any policy development. Strategy 5 calls for Governments to consider ratifying the core international human rights treaties. Strategy 6 calls for Governments to consider support for the Ad Hoc Committee for the comprehensive and integral international convention to promote and protect the rights and dignity of persons with disabilities. Strategy 7 calls on Governments to include persons with disabilities and their organizations, in their procedures at the national, regional and international levels, concerning the drafting and adoption of the proposed human rights convention on disability.

Disability statistics/common definition of disabilities for planning

A common system of definition and classification of disability is not uniformly applied in the region. Two strategies are set to solve the problem. Strategy 8 calls for Governments to develop, by 2005, their system in disability-related data collection and analysis. Strategy 9 calls for Governments to adopt, by 2005, definitions on disability based on the United Nations publication "Guidelines and Principles for the Development of Disability Statistics.

Strengthened community development approach to prevention, rehabilitation and empowerment of persons with disabilities

The community-based approach is augmenting and replacing traditional institutional and centralized rehabilitation programmes for disabled people's economic, social and other human rights enhancement. Strategy 10 calls for Governments to immediately develop national policies to promote community-based approaches.

Cooperation and support for action: subregional, regional and interregional

A special focus is on strengthening cooperation among governments at the subregional level. Strategies 11 and 12 call for developing subregional mechanisms, by 2004, to achieve the targets. At a regional level, strategy 13 calls for Governments, the United Nations system, civil society organizations and the private sector to collaborate, support and take advantage of the training and communication capability of the Asia-Pacific Development Center on Disability. This centre is to be opened in 2004 in Bangkok, as a legacy of the Asian and Pacific Decade of Disabled Persons. It has the capacity to be one of the most powerful focal points in the region. Strategies 14 and 15 call for Governments, civil society organizations and the private sector to establish a network of centres of excellence in focused areas to maximize cooperation and collaboration. ESCAP and other United Nations agencies should assist in the establishment of a network of centres of excellence. Strategy 16 calls for a suitable agreement on trade, technology transfer and human resource development for fast and efficient sharing of resources. Strategy 17 proposes that the Asian and Pacific region, the African region and the Western Asian region should strengthen their cooperation and collaboration to create synergy in implementing regional decades through interregional exchange of information, experiences and expertise, which will mutually benefit all the regions.

Monitoring and review

ESCAP should convene biennial meetings to review achievements and to identify actions that may be required to implement the Biwako Millennium Framework for Action. At these meetings, the representatives of national coordination committees on disability matters comprising Government ministries/agencies, NGOs, self-help organizations and the media will be invited to present reports to review progress in the implementation of the framework.

A mid-point review of the Biwako Millennium Framework for Action should be conducted. Based on the review, the targets and strategic plans for the second half of the Decade may be modified and new targets and strategic plans formulated.

The Trust Fund for the Decade

Background

In 1992, the concluding year of the United Nations Decade of Disabled Persons, the United Nations Economic and Social Commission for Asia and the Pacific (ESCAP) proclaimed the period 1993-2002 as the Asian and Pacific Decade of Disabled Persons. The theme of the Asian and Pacific Decade was the *promotion of the full participation and equality of people with disabilities*.

In December 1992, ESCAP convened at Beijing a Meeting to Launch the Asian and Pacific Decade of Disabled Persons, 1993-2002. The Meeting formulated an Agenda for Action for the Asian and Pacific Decade of Disabled Persons (hereinafter referred to as the Decade Agenda for Action). At its forty-ninth session in April 1993, the Commission adopted the Decade Agenda for Action.

ESCAP subsequently established a Fund for the Asian and Pacific Decade of Disabled Persons, 1993-2002, with pledges and contributions from several ESCAP members and associate members in support of Decade activities, as delineated in the Decade Agenda for Action.

The Fund was extended for the period of the New Decade, 2003-2012.

Purpose of the Fund for the Decade

The Fund is designed to strengthen the building of capacity to enable persons with disabilities to fulfil their potential for participating in society, in order for them to break out of the vicious cycle of poverty associated with disability, and to support the breaking of social and physical barriers that marginalize persons with disabilities from participation in mainstream community life.

Activities Supported

The Fund is intended to promote intercountry cooperation and facilitate implementation, by ESCAP developing countries and territories, concerning the BMF under the new Decade, through: technical exchange, training and information dissemination using "best practices"; and advisory services by experts drawn from the ESCAP region.

Emphasis will be given to building capacity and strengthening capabilities for:

- National- and local-level implementation of the Biwako targets, with special attention to the active participation of self-help organizations and women with disabilities;

- National and sub national coordination of disability-related actions, especially with regard to multisectoral collaborative action to include persons with disabilities in mainstream development programmes, including those for education and training, rural and urban development, the International Convention, disability statistics, employment and gender equality;

- Promotion of accessible ICT and access to information;

- Promotion of non-handicapping environments and equalization legislation for persons with disabilities.

Some donors

Australia; Brunei Darussalam; Cambodia; China; Hong Kong, China; India; Indonesia; Republic of Korea; Singapore; Thailand; Honda Motor Workers' Union; and others

Your contributions to the Fund

Your contribution to the Fund is highly appreciated. Those who wish to contribute are kindly invited to contact us:

Population and Social Integration Section
Emerging Social Issues Division

Phone: (662) 288-1590
Fax: (662) 288-1030
E-mail: escap-esid-psis@un.org